THE MAKIN... DSCAPE

Other titles of interest in the West Yorkshire area

THE MAKING OF THE
WEST YORKSHIRE LANDSCAPE

A popular guide to the history of the county's countryside and townscapes

Anthony Silson

WITH LINE ILLUSTRATIONS BY TREVOR PLOWS

Wharncliffe Books

To Margaret and Judith

09342458

**First Published in 2003 by
Wharncliffe Books
an imprint of
Pen and Sword Books Limited,
47 Church Street, Barnsley,
South Yorkshire. S70 2AS**

Copyright © Anthony Silson, 2003

*For up-to-date information on other titles produced under the
Wharncliffe imprint, please telephone or write to:*

**Wharncliffe Books
FREEPOST
47 Church Street
Barnsley
South Yorkshire S70 2BR
Telephone (24 hours): 01226 - 734555**

ISBN: 1-903425-31-X

A CIP catalogue record of this book is available from the
British Library

Cover illustrations:
Front: Priesthorpe Lane, Farsley
Back: (clockwise from top left) Keighley Moor, Burmantofts, Darrington Church, The Holme valley, The People's Park.

Printed in Great Britain by
CPI UK

CONTENTS

All photographs are taken by the author except where indicated.

ACKNOWLEDGEMENTS

First and foremost, my thanks must go to my close friends Margaret Plows and Trevor Plows who, through their constant encouragement and help, have contributed so much to this book. Margaret not only typed my barely legible long hand, but read, and made constructive comments on, each chapter. Trevor took my rough maps and diagrams and transformed them into the splendid form visible here. Next, I must thank the large number of private individuals, church members and people who run small businesses who have so readily answered my many questions. I would also like to thank various local council employees, including librarians, and staff at each of the following: the West Yorkshire Archaeology Service, Bramham Park, the West Yorkshire Sculpture Park, the Henry Moore Foundation and DEFRA. The Thoresby Society has been a valued source for many books.

This book was written between 2001 and 2003, but to a degree, it is the product of a lifetime of scholarship, and hence it is appropriate to identify, and to thank, some of the people who have influenced my interests, concepts and knowledge. L.D. Stamp's little book, *The Face of Britain*, Longmans Green, 1944 stimulated my exploration of the British countryside. W. Christaller, H. C. Darby, D. Linton, A. E. Smailes, W. Smith and S. W. Wooldridge are a mere half dozen of the countless other writers who have developed my understanding of the landscape. Almost sixty years ago, Miss Smith gave me my first formal lessons in history and geography, and awarded me a little book on the Arctic. Other teachers who taught and influenced me in my youth include W. A. Griffiths, Oswald Harland, Richard Lawton and H. R. Wilkinson. Much later in life, Diane Exley widened my grasp of local history. My thanks must also go to my dog for his companionship and adaptability on countless, but essential, field trips made through the length and breadth of West Yorkshire. Finally, though they are now deceased, I record my thanks to my uncle, Sydney Tiffany MBE who, being largely self-educated, created an atmosphere that learning mattered, and my parents who allowed me to study well beyond the then usual school leaving age. My mother not only introduced me to parts of West Yorkshire that lay beyond our home, but allowed me, on my own and from the age of five, to explore our neighbourhood.

Anthony Silson
Bramley, June 2003

A DIVERSE AND EVER CHANGING LANDSCAPE

COCKERS DALE POSSESSES a pronounced rural aspect with green fields in its upper reaches and dense woodland downstream. Above all, the dale is so secluded that a rambler can readily believe it is located in the very heart of the countryside. Nothing could be further from the truth. Barely a kilometre to the east lies the overgrown commuter village of Gildersome and, next to it, an industrial estate. Yet taken together, Cockers Dale and Gildersome exemplify the diversity and the rapidity of change that characterise so much of the landscape of the county of West Yorkshire.

OBSERVING A LANDSCAPE

People perceive a particular landscape in different ways. A botanist or a painter might focus upon a single flower or tree,

Figure 1.1. *The landscape from Norland Moor looking north west up the Calder valley.*

but the approach adopted here is to emphasise groups rather than individuals; woodland say, rather than one tree. Moreover, particular attention is paid to those groups of features that either differ from place to place or form distinct spatial patterns. The landscape west of Norland Moor, near Sowerby Bridge, has been chosen to illustrate how a landscape may be observed (Figure 1.1). Patches of bare rock mark the edge of Norland Moor which falls steeply to a gently sloping surface. Beyond, and partly tucked away, lies a deep, steep sided valley which, on its further side, rises as a moderately angled spur. The small part of Norland Moor that is visible is covered in heather and rough grass. Straight-edged, moderate sized fields are visible, and although one field appears to be in rough grass, the other fields are covered with improved grass. Woodland occurs on the valley sides. Houses lie scattered amongst the fields; beyond, a large cluster of houses could be either a large village or a small town. A road connects the scattered houses.

Fields, plant cover, transport, houses, villages and towns are some of the main features that make up the human landscape of an area. The physical landscape includes an area's slopes, rivers and streams.

Whilst observation is important, it is but a part of landscape interpretation. This book aims to help the reader acquire some understanding of how people's activities, at different periods of time, have contributed to the contemporary landscape. Physical processes have also played an important part in the making of the landscape. In the Norland area, a spatial relationship exists between the physical and human features of the landscape. Woodland occupies the steep sides of the distant valley. The lower gentle slopes are occupied by enclosed farmland and scattered houses, whilst the higher gentle slopes have a moorland cover. Between the two is a steep slope with some bare rock which, though this cannot be established from the photograph, is partly the remains of former quarrying. Detailed spatial relationships between the physical and human landscapes are quite common; a second illustration can be seen near Wentbridge (Figure 1.4). At the county scale, spatial relationships are not always so clear cut, but broad contrasts certainly exist in each of the physical and human landscapes.

DIVERSITIES IN THE PHYSICAL LANDSCAPE AND ENVIRONMENT

Major contrasts in the physical landscape occur between the Pennines and the lowlands that adjoin them in the east (Figure 1.2a). Many Pennine spur and ridge tops are gently sloping, a property which in no small measure contributes to the area's numerous panoramas. Although, in the extreme

south west, an altitude of 582 metres is reached at Black Hill, most of the gently sloping surfaces in the western Pennines lie at heights between 400 and 520 metres. In the eastern Pennines, gently sloping surfaces occur at lower heights particularly at about 200 metres. All these surfaces are deeply dissected by steep sided valleys which even the urban veneers of Halifax and Huddersfield cannot disguise. The eastern lowlands are characterised by rolling, gentle slopes, but unlike those of the Pennines, their summits scarcely reach one hundred metres in altitude. Consequently, the valleys dissecting the eastern lowlands are far less deep than those of the Pennines. Escarpments occur in both areas, but they are more common in the Pennines (Figure 1.3). The only major scarp in the lowlands is low, but bold, and runs between Pontefract and Wentbridge (Figure 1.4).

Climate often varies with altitude in West Yorkshire. Spring comes later and autumn begins earlier at high altitudes so the length of the growing season is shortened. However, below

Figure 1.2. *(a) West Yorkshire: physical landscape regions and geology. (b) West Yorkshire: main human landscape divisions.*

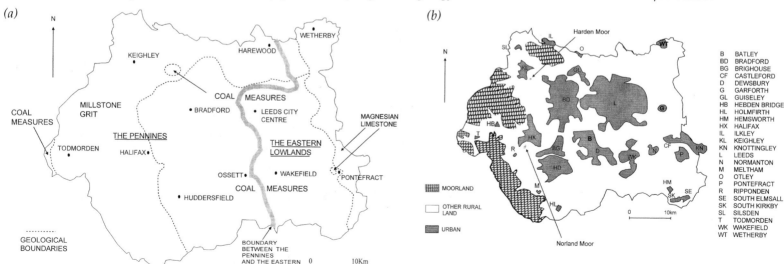

Figure 1.3. Scarps to the east of Hepworth. The main scarp is visible near the horizon; notice the depth of the whole valley.

altitudes of about 230 metres, there is but little variation in temperature with height and, at these lower elevations, winters are cool (with mean January temperatures close to three degrees Celsius) and summers are warm (with mean July temperatures of about sixteen degrees Celsius). There are, though, very great increases in mean annual rainfall as height increases. Winds frequently blow from westerly directions so the western Pennines receive most rainfall. In the extreme south west this amounts to over 1600 millimetres, but the amount decreases to about 1000 millimetres in the north west. This difference not only arises because the north west is lower

than the south west, but because the north west is sheltered by the Forest of Rossendale (in Lancashire) whereas no such shelter occurs, under westerly winds, in the south west. Mean annual rainfall decreases down the eastern slopes of the Pennines, and it becomes really dry in the southern part of the eastern lowlands where most places receive only between 600 and 650 millimetres.

The low rainfall and the warm summers of the eastern lowlands create soil moisture deficits in the summer months. These deficits are intensified, in the extreme east, by the presence of porous Magnesian Limestone, which is composed of Magnesium Carbonate and Calcium Carbonate. Limestone soils are thin, but have a crumb structure which retains nutrients for plant growth. The soil type that forms most frequently on Magnesian Limestone is called brown

Figure 1.4. Plain and scarp near Wentbridge.

calcareous; it was highly valued by prehistoric people, and today it is the best quality farmland in the county.

West of the Magnesian Limestone, the solid rocks are either Coal Measures or Millstone Grit (Figure 1.2(a)). Millstone Grit not only has beds of grit, but beds of sandstone and shale. Gritstones consist of coarse sand particles cemented together; sandstones are more finely grained whilst shale is composed of the finest, clay sized, rock particles. The rock particles in shale occur in very narrow layers which can be easily split. The Coal Measures consist of beds of sandstone, shale, coal seams and ironstone.

In places gritstone is overlain by a soil known as a podsol. These are infertile soils, and many have a hard pan, lower down the profile, which impedes drainage and thereby promotes peat growth on the surface. Peat occurs widely in the higher parts of the Pennines. In other instances, gritstone, along with sandstone, promotes the formation of brown earths. These soils are made up of layers of different shades of brown. They are well drained, and this contributes to their rather acid nature. The solid rocks in parts of West Yorkshire, particularly in the north, are overlain by recent loose rock some of which is clay. Shale and clay are often badly drained, and, on average, the water table lies near the surface. In dry spells, when the water table falls a little, iron in the soil is oxidised and possesses a reddish brown colour; in wet spells, the water table rises and iron is reduced and becomes bluish-green. As a result, the soils become mottled, and are then called gley soils. The role of gley, brown earths and brown calcareous soils in the farmed landscape is examined in chapter nine.

A DIVERSE HUMAN LANDSCAPE
The far west of the Pennines are distinguished by patches of moorland which may be small as at Harden Moor and Norland Moor, or far more extensive as happens to the south west of Keighley (Figure 1.2(b)). As the crow flies, some moorland may be but a short distance from a railway or busy road, but, be under no illusions, most of the moors are desolate places, devoid of settlement, where it is possible to walk for hours and not meet a soul. This is not to imply the moorlands are unused; far from it. Apart from the moors' value for rambling, lines of shooting butts, which cross some of the northern moors, testify to their use for grouse shooting, and many parts of the moors and their margins are occupied by reservoirs, constructed mainly to supply water to towns (Figure 1.5).

Downslope and, usually, eastward, the moors abruptly give way to improved grassland enclosed by stone walls. Likewise, most buildings are made of stone. That apart, settlement is remarkably varied and ranges from solitary farmhouses to

Figure 1.5. Shooting butt on Oakworth Moor.

small towns. Many villages, including Farnley Tyas, Heptonstall and Stanbury, occupy dry sites, elevated well above rivers. Yet other villages, including Oxenhope, Marsden and Walsden, are sited in, or close to, valley floors, alongside the mills which have contributed to their growth. Sometimes houses spread upslope from the valley floor, a circumstance particularly evident at New Mill where part of the village occupies a tributary valley. The towns (Figure 1.2(b)) are located in, or near, valley floors, and their form is greatly influenced by the gradient of the valley sides. At Silsden, the valley sides have gentle to moderate gradients, so the buildings have spread out from the Leeds and Liverpool Canal to form an almost semi-circular plan. In contrast, at Todmorden very steep valley sides restrict building and give the town an almost straight edged branched plan. Many of these small Pennine towns may be only a little larger than villages, but they are distinguished from them by possessing a centre with a varied range of services that include a town hall and/or market.

These mainly small towns are outliers of a vast area dominated by urban landscapes in the central eastern Pennines (Figure 1.2(b)). Large parts of these urban areas are occupied by houses, but they are varied by the presence of parks and by several service centres where pedestrian flows are often high (Figure 1.6). On the edges of the several towns that comprise this vast urban sprawl is a very mixed landscape that includes golf courses, houses, works and farmland. Some farms grow crops, other than grass, and many fields are divided by hedgerows.

The east side of Leeds spills out on to the eastern lowlands. An almost continuous stretch of urban landscape, but smaller than that in the Pennines, extends from Wakefield, through Normanton and Castleford to Knottingley and Pontefract. The

Figure 1.6. The market cross, Central Huddersfield.

towns of Wetherby and Hemsworth have similar services to the small Pennine towns, but Hemsworth is distinguished by possessing a higher proportion of brick buildings. Despite its urban areas, most of the eastern lowlands is rural with substantial areas of cropland (Figure 1.4). The fields are usually larger than those in the Pennines, and hedges are more typical than stone walls. The area is dotted with scattered houses and numerous large villages. Some of these possess Anglo-Saxon churches, but most houses date from the twentieth century for the villages are either, in the north, chiefly commuter villages, or, on the Coal Measures in the south, former mining villages, many of which now have their commuter components. Former mining villages usually include terraced and/or council houses and an actual or former working men's club. Wherever the Coal Measures occur (Figure 1.2(a)), former mining has left its mark on the landscape, but its effects have been greatest in the south eastern lowlands where mining has been most recent and most extensive. Even in the south east, some villages, including Wentbridge in its cosy woodland setting, were aloof from mining, and have a very different character to the former mining villages. Appreciable parts of the eastern lowlands are wooded, and some of the woods are located in the park lands of country houses. Two of the best known of these are Bramham and Nostell Priory.

AN EVER CHANGING LANDSCAPE

Within the last 7,000 years, people have played a key role in landscape change. In some places one human landscape has been completely replaced by another; elsewhere, change has been less complete, and traces of former landscapes are visible.

At a canal side site in Rodley, Leeds, replacement has occurred not once, but twice within the last couple of centuries. The first landscape replacement took place between 1831 and the early twentieth century, when a field was gradually occupied by a large foundry and crane works. Business ceased in the 1980s, and the premises remained empty until 1999. Between that year and 2002, the works were demolished, and have been so completely replaced by residential and office accommodation that no sign of the old crane works remain (Figure 1.7).

Roundhay Park, Leeds, illustrates how a landscape may consist of features created at different historical times.

Medieval Roundhay had been a woodland, but by the end of the eighteenth century, most of the woodland had been cleared and converted to farmland. The gorge, though, remained wooded as it still does to the present day. In the early nineteenth century, Thomas Nicholson bought the land, and converted the farmland into a park of grass and scattered trees. Waterloo Lake and an upper lake were formed in two valleys. To the west of Nicholson's Mansion House, the canal gardens were created. A folly, in the form of a castle, was erected shortly after Thomas had died, when the estate was held by Stephen Nicholson. Leeds City Council acquired the park in 1872, but all the features made by the Nicholsons have been retained. The Council has merely modified Nicholsons' landscape,

principally to provide opportunities for sports and games; for example, a sports arena was made below the Mansion House, but without ruining the vista.

The types of change that have occurred at Rodley and Roundhay are but a part of county wide landscape changes. Some seven thousand years ago, people began to clear the well wooded landscape. Clearances were initially made to extend the grazing area, but were later required for crop growth. In the Iron Age, houses lay scattered amongst enclosed fields, but at some time between 900 and 1300, the farmed landscape was re-organised into open fields and villages. Enclosed landscapes probably never fully disappeared, and, from about 1500, the number of enclosed fields increased either through reclamation of waste, for there was then relatively little woodland left, or by the enclosure of open fields. By the mid-nineteenth century, villages remained, but the open fields were no more.

The period between 1780 and 1918 not only saw the demise of open fields, but witnessed very great changes in transport, industry and towns. Turnpike roads, canals and railways, spread across the county. New mines, mills and factories sprang up, and there were great increases in the population size of many towns including Leeds, Bradford and Huddersfield.

Between 1918 and 2003, manufacturing has declined and mining has effectively ceased. Motorways have been built, and their presence has encouraged the growth of commercial premises just beyond some of the urban areas. Perhaps the greatest change of all has been the enormous outward growth of urban areas in the

Figure 1.7. (left) The Union Crane Works, Rodley, 1998. (above) The same site, 2002.

central part of the county, so that it is now hard to see where one town ends and another begins.

These great changes, along with more detailed ones, are examined more fully in chapters two to six. The second half of the book examines the relative significance of continuity and replacement in the contemporary landscape. Within that half of the book, rural and urban landscapes are discussed separately, and the book concludes with three chapters discussing features which occur both in rural and urban areas.

Some Sources and Further Reading

MAPS

1:250,000 *Sheet 1 Northern England, Soils of England and Wales*, Soil Survey of England and Wales, 1983.

1:400,000 *Scapes and Fringes*. Second Land Utilisation Survey of Britain, n/d.

1:625,000 *Geological Map of England and Wales*, Geological Survey, 1948.

1:625,000 *Average Annual Rainfall, Southern Britain Sheet*, Meteorological Office, 1977.

BOOKS

DODGSHON, R. A. and BUTLIN, R. A. *An Historical Geography of England and Wales*, Academic Press, 1995. Useful for anyone wishing to set West Yorkshire within the context of England and Wales.

RAISTRICK, A. *West Riding of Yorkshire*, Hodder and Stoughton, 1970. As the title indicates, this covers the whole of the former West Riding of Yorkshire, a much larger area than the present county of West Yorkshire.

SLACK, M. *Portrait of West Yorkshire*, Robert Hale, 1984. This interesting book has a wider brief than landscape history.

Places to Visit

Many of the places mentioned in this book are accessible by car or public transport, but in some instances they are best, or only to be, viewed on foot. Perhaps it is worth reminding those who walk that, particularly in moorland areas, they may encounter adverse weather conditions.

If you intend to explore West Yorkshire on foot, you should own a copy of the 1:25,000 Ordnance Survey *Explorer Series sheets OL21, 278, 288, 289 and 297.*

A sound impression of the variety of landscapes to be found within the county can be obtained by making a train journey from **Walsden** to **Micklefield**. Highlights of the journey include Todmorden Unitarian Church, Stoodley Pike Monument, between Sowerby Bridge and Halifax Wainhouse Tower, Halifax former Square Church and St John the Baptist Church, Lightcliffe former Congregational Church, Bradford City Hall, Leeds Third White Cloth Hall and Leeds Parish Church. An alternative rail journey between **South Elmsall** and **Ilkley** gives an equally good general impression of the main landscape contrasts. Perhaps it has fewer individual highlights, but Wakefield Cathedral can be seen, and there are good views of Kirkstall Abbey.

WEST YORKSHIRE TAKES SHAPE

WEST YORKSHIRE'S LANDSCAPES have been in the making for millions of years. For almost all that time, the landscape has been shaped by natural processes. Agents of erosion at some time planed the land to produce the many stretches of gently sloping, upland surfaces visible today. Valley forms have been influenced by differences in rock type and changes in climate, but they have also been influenced by human beings.

CHANGES IN LANDFORMS FROM ONE HUNDRED MILLION TO TWO MILLION YEARS AGO

Almost one hundred million years ago, the sea advanced over the whole of what would become West Yorkshire, and, as it did so, waves trimmed the area to an extensive platform on which younger rocks were then deposited. Some sixty five million years ago, the sea withdrew to reveal an easterly sloping area of recently deposited rocks. The Aire and Calder began to flow eastwards across, and into, this newly formed land, but the Wharfe, from near what became Wetherby, flowed north eastwards. These rivers transported the recently deposited rocks eastwards to the North Sea. Eventually this allowed these rivers to erode into the former wave trimmed platform. From sixty-five to forty million years ago, West Yorkshire experienced a tropical climate that led to very deeply weathered rocks. These rocks were then removed by surface wash and rivers which, in time, might have been expected to produce a new plain. However, this prolonged tropical period and a later cooler, but still often warm, period coincided with frequent movements of the earth which probably inhibited the formation of extensive plains.

It was not until times were rather more stable, perhaps scarcely five million years ago, that an extensive plain was produced by weathering and erosion. By then, the climate, although warm, was much cooler than it had been fifty million years ago, with the consequence that weathered rock was far less deep. Relatively, therefore, other agents of denudation, such as rivers and surface wash, assumed greater importance in the formation of this plain.

The gently sloping surfaces, at heights of between about 400 and 520 metres, that are so characteristic of the western Pennines today, are composed of peat between one and nine

Figure 2.1. The almost even skyline is a bed of peat that probably overlies part of an erosion surface c.400-520 metres in height. The photograph shows the view south westwards from near Leeshaw Reservoir, Haworth, to Top of Stairs.

metres deep. It is believed that the peat lies on gently sloping solid rock surfaces and, if this is the case, these surfaces may be remnants of the extensive plain produced by erosion within the last five million years (Figure 2.1). The plain was then elevated either by sea level falling, perhaps as a result of subsidence in a North Sea basin, or by the land rising. As a result of this overall uplift, rivers acquired renewed energy to cut downwards, so dissecting the plain into fragments, producing steep valley sides and, in some places, scarps. It may have been at this time that the whole of the southern Pennines began to appear as a distinct upland, rising above lower land, through the combined actions of uplift and the more rapid erosion of less resistant rock on either side of the Pennines.

Uplift seems to have been intermittent, allowing time for at least one lower, but much narrower, plain to form, remnants of which are now visible as valley side benches. About 2.4 million years ago, when the ice age was beginning, the broad outlines of the relief of West Yorkshire were in place, but the sea level was at a height of 217 metres. In the eastern Pennines, waves in this sea eroded a platform, with heights ranging from 183 to 217 metres, that can be seen between Drighlington and East Bierley today. During the ice age, sea level fluctuated, but overall the level fell. There were, though, periods when the sea level remained at one height for a sufficiently long period for lower wave cut platforms to be formed.

This chronology is an attempt to synthesise pre-1960s findings with more recent concepts. It is a field of study where there is great uncertainty, particularly with regard to how many erosion surfaces exist, when they were formed and how erosion actually produced them.

ROCKS, RIVERS AND RELIEF
A high degree of certainty exists about the origin of waterfalls and scarps. Each is a consequence of different types of rock

Figure 2.2. Lumb Falls. (a) Their appearance, (b) their origin.

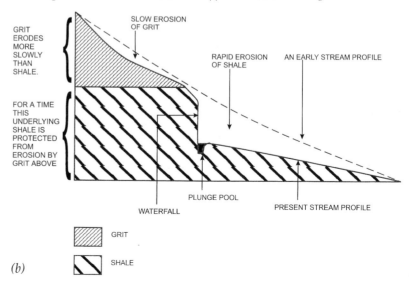

(a)

(b)

eroding at different rates, but whilst waterfalls are mere pin pricks in the landscape, scarps are some of its major components. Amongst West Yorkshire's finest falls are Goit Stock Waterfall on Harden Beck and Lumb Falls in Crimsworth Dean. Visually, the latter is enhanced by a packhorse bridge very slightly up stream of the falls. Each of the falls has a small plunge pool and steep valley sides in front of the fall (Figure 2.2a). Both falls owe their existence to a bed of grit resting upon less resistant shale located where the stream is actively eroding downwards (Figure 2.2b).

With a few exceptions, such as Thornhill Edge, most scarps are a part of westward facing valley sides that, from their summits, slope gently down towards the east. One well-defined scarp runs south east from Pontefract (Figure 1.4) whilst others occur frequently in the eastern Pennines. Of the Airedale scarps, that which runs from Cockers Dale into Troy Dale is particularly fine, and the scarp is so steep at Post Hill that it has been used for motorcycle scrambles. The north-south trending valleys between Huddersfield and Hepworth have lengthy stretches of west facing scarps (Figure 1.3). Scarps

Figure 2.3. The appearance and formation of a scarp in the Hebble Valley.

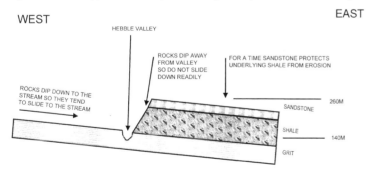

are also common features on the west facing sides of the tributaries of the Calder (Figure 2.3). The essential conditions for a scarp to form are that the dip of the rocks must be either horizontal or away from the valley side and for a more resistant cap rock to lie above less resistant rock (Figure 2.3). Usually the less resistant rock is shale and the cap rock is grit or sandstone, but the Pontefract scarp has a cap rock of Magnesian Limestone and the scarp face is Ackworth Rock (a sandstone). However, to the west of the Pontefract scarp, the Ackworth Rock forms the low hills and shale the plains.

Many West Yorkshire valley sides have a stepped appearance in which a lower steep slope gives way to a gentle slope before again rising steeply. Heptonstall is sited on such a bench, well above the flood prone Calder valley floor. Many benches have a grit or sandstone surface with the steeper slope consisting of shale, but some benches may have been cut in relation to a higher sea level than that of today, and then, when the sea level fell, the river cut downwards leaving its former floor as benches. Where a flight of such benches occur, they may relate to a flight of marine platforms (previous section).

THE IMPACT OF GLACIERS

Look across the Aire valley from the Druid's Altar, or some similar elevated spot between Shipley and Keighley, and try to imagine the valley when it was occupied by a glacier a mere seventeen thousand years ago. It is not as easy as it seems, but the evidence for the former presence of a glacier is compelling. Rather surprisingly, the evidence includes three belts of low hummocky hills that lie across the Aire valley at Hirst Wood, Bingley and Utley. These hills consist of rock that could not have been deposited from rivers, in the sea or by the wind, but they do resemble rock found at the snout (down valley end) of many existing glaciers. The three belts of low hills are called end moraines, and they were formed during the most recent of two occasions when West Yorkshire experienced a climate so cold that parts were occupied by glaciers.

The end moraine at Hirst Wood is one of the three places where the Airedale glacier's snout scarcely moved for a large number of years (Figure 2.4). Year after year the glacier conveyed a supply of various sized rock fragments down valley, but at its snout, meltwater was unable to transport the larger fragments, so these remained to build a low ridge across the valley. A period of rapid warming followed, the lower part of the glacier melted away and the snout occupied a new position at Bingley. For a number of years there was no further

warming, so the snout remained at Bingley, and an end moraine formed there. Another period of rapid warming, followed by a period of stability, led to a further moraine forming at Utley. Down valley from Hirst Wood, end moraines occur at Tong Park and Apperley Bridge, but both may have been formed by a glacier moving from Wharfedale, through the Guiseley Gap into Airedale, rather than by an Airedale glacier. In the Wharfe valley, end moraines formed at Arthington, and between Ilkley and Addingham.

Behind the end moraines at Hirst Wood, Bingley and Utley, short-lived lakes formed, and though these have long since

Figure 2.4. Some former glacial features in Airedale.

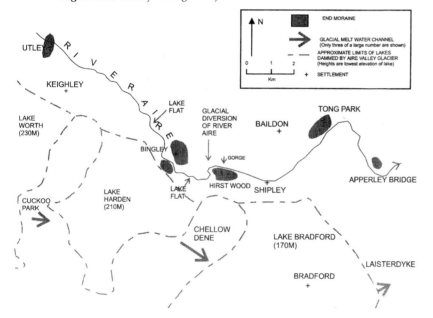

Figure 2.5. Former meltwater channel at Walsden looking north to Dobroyd Castle. The dry valley floor was followed by the Rochdale Canal and the Manchester and Leeds Railway.

drained away, they have left a legacy of flat valley floors above the moraine. The Airedale glacier itself dammed southern tributary valleys, and so these also became lakes. Water escaped from these lakes and cut steep sided valleys known as meltwater channels. As the climate became warmer, the Aire glacier melted away and so these lakes drained, and the melt water channels are now left as dry valleys. A fine example of a former meltwater channel runs from Littleborough, via Walsden, to Todmorden, but in this instance, meltwater came from ice that lay to the south west of Rochdale (Figure 2.5). Occasionally, though, drainage has been permanently changed. At Wetherby, the River Wharfe has been diverted from flowing north eastwards to flowing towards the south east (Figure 2.6).

The cross profiles of the Aire and Wharfe valleys have also been changed by glacial action. The dimensions of the channels of the Aire and Wharfe glaciers were many times greater than the channels of the rivers today. Consequently, these valleys were deepened and widened by glacial erosion. The channel walls were kept almost vertical by the presence of the glaciers, but once these had melted, the walls were no longer supported. Landslips occurred, being particularly evident below Otley Chevin, and so the valley sides are no longer as steep as when a glacier was present, though they are still steep.

The Calder valley was not occupied by a glacier during the new glaciation, so its shape is very different from those of the Aire and the Wharfe. There are no end moraines to diversify the Calder valley which, within its Pennine section, has a very narrow floor. Meltwater, from Lancashire, contributed to the formation of the very steep lower valley sides in the Pennine part of the Calder valley.

RECENT CHANGES IN CLIMATE AND LANDFORMS

By thirteen thousand years ago, a rise in temperature had freed West Yorkshire of its glaciers. Indeed, for a time, it was probably warm enough for forests to grow, but, as so often has been the case in the last two million years, there was yet another rapid change in climate, and between eleven thousand and ten thousand years ago, the climate was so cold that glaciers re-advanced in the Lake District. During this cold spell, tors (isolated rocks pedestals) such as Doubler Stones and Great Bride Stones formed (Figure 2.7). These tors are made of grit that is particularly liable to weathering along its joints (cracks). The density of joints varies, and where high density joints occur, weathering is far more rapid than at places with low density joints. Hence a core of rock becomes surrounded by very well broken rock. When the latter is transported downslope, the core stands up as a tor. It is highly likely that repeated night time freezing broke up the rock and daytime

Figure 2.6. *Stages in the diversion of the River Wharfe at Wetherby.*

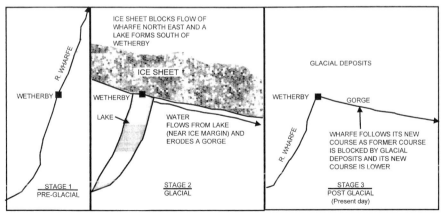

Figure 2.7. A tor at Great Bride Stones, near Todmorden.

Figure 2.8. A river terrace between Ilkley and Addingham. The lowest land is the flood plain. The terrace rises near the silage bags, and the house is built on the terrace.

meltwater transported the broken rock away. However, some geomorphologists believe tors formed when the climate was much warmer than today, perhaps even before the oldest glaciation.

Parts of Addingham, Ilkley, Burley in Wharfedale, Pool and Collingham are built on terraces near the River Wharfe and parts of Keighley, Methley, Mickletown and Allerton Bywater are built on terraces close to the River Aire (Figure 2.8). Terraces are gently sloping deposits of rock elevated above a valley floor by a steep slope, and they, therefore, offer dry sites above a floodplain. Many of the Wharfe terraces consist of rock deposited from the meltwater of glaciers; other terraces are made of alluvium deposited by rivers. These deposits were then dissected by rivers, so they are now elevated above the present valley floor.

THE EFFECTS OF PEOPLE ON LANDFORMS

Natural processes continue to shape the land today, but people have also influenced contemporary landforms. Peat, that blankets many higher parts of the Pennines, was once thought to have formed solely by a substantial increase in yearly rainfall that began c.5000 BC. It is now believed that later

Mesolithic, Neolithic and Bronze Age people, when they cleared upland woodland either by burning or felling, played a key role in peat formation. Peat forms when a soil becomes waterlogged. With the loss of a tree cover, a hard pan forms in some upland soils, and rain water more readily penetrates as far as the pan, hence waterlogging develops above the pan. Today parts of the peat retain an even surface, but large parts are dissected. Some of the peat has been eroded by streams, but much of the peat has been cut by people needing fuel; Hades Peat Pits were worked for this purpose until the end of the nineteenth century.

Cuttings have also been made in solid rock. In the nineteenth century, a magnificent cutting, that bears some resemblance to a limestone gorge, was made to provide an impressive setting for the approaches to Ferncliffe House, Calverley. Indeed the provision of transport has widely affected the land forms of West Yorkshire. Whilst the basins of ox bow lakes are former river meanders, the change from meander to lake has, in many instances, been a result of eighteenth and nineteenth century river straightening to improve navigation (chapter five). Embankments have been made to create gentle gradients for railways, but they have also been made to form reservoirs. Some reservoirs were made to feed canals, but others were built to supply water to mills and towns and cities.

Former shallow coal and iron ore mining has left its mark in the Pennines in the form of sporadic mounds (Figure 4.3). Deep quarries have also been dug in the Pennines, but some of these have later been infilled so that the former quarry is now flat.

The landforms of parts of the coalfield section of the eastern lowlands have been modified by human activity over the last half century. Some shallow, marshy hollows, such as those at Bottom Boat, have been infilled with ash and colliery waste to form a small plateau, and similar mining waste forms the

impressive hill, currently being landscaped, immediately north of St Aidan's open cast working (Figure 8.4). Deep mining has led to surface subsidence in a number of places; the lakes that lie immediately to the east of Pit Lane, Mickletown, have formed as a consequence of such subsidence. Many basins formed by open cast mining have been restored, but, to the south of Wakefield, the lakes at Pugneys and Anglers Country Parks occupy former open cast workings.

MESOLITHIC PEOPLE

The cold spell, during which tors probably developed, was very short-lived, and by 7500 BC the climate had again become warm enough for birch and hazel woodlands to flourish. Between the approximate dates of 6500 BC and 5000 BC, the climate was drier and warmer than that of today, and this led to widespread oak forests. In these forests very small patches of open land occurred near rivers or where the wind had blown trees over. Wild horses and oxen grazed in these glades, whilst deer, pigs and wolves foraged in the sheltered wooded areas. It is during this period that the first certain traces of human beings occur in West Yorkshire. These earlier Mesolithic (middle stone age) people hunted wild animals. Slain deer provided them with bone and antler tools, and they also used broad stone blades about forty millimetres long.

Between approximately 5000 BC and 3500 BC, different communities of deciduous forest became established with oak dominant on the Pennines, lime on the lowlands and ash on the Magnesian Limestone. These forests flourished under a climate that was both warmer and wetter than that of today.

Patches of forest were locally cleared by later Mesolithic people who inhabited the county from approximately 5000 BC to 3500 BC. Later Mesolithic peoples did not use bone and antler implements, and the blades they used were narrow with sharp points. Fruit and hazel nuts were gathered and wild animals were hunted. Hunting was probably a collective activity in which a tribe formed a rough circle around a beast. Stone blades attached to wooden shafts were then flung at the animal. It is quite likely that relatively permanent camps were established on dry sites above marshy floodplains. With the warmer climate of those years, temporary hunting camps were probably established at higher elevations during the summer. Fires were used to create extra grazing land and to drive wild animals together, so making them easier to kill. Through their use of fire, later Mesolithic people extended the small area of open land and in this way began to create West Yorkshire's moorland.

Some Sources and Further Reading

BERESFORD, M. W. and JONES, G. R. J. *Leeds And Its Region*, Leeds Local Executive Committee of the British Association for the Advancement of Science, 1967.

BRITISH GEOLOGICAL SURVEY *1:50,000 Geology Maps, 69,70,77,78,86 (Solid and Drift)*, Ordnance Survey.

EDWARDS, W. et al *Geology of the District North and East of Leeds*, HMSO, 1950.

GOUDIE, A. S. *The landforms of England and Wales*, Blackwell, 1990.

GOUDIE, A. S. and BRUNSDEN, D. *The Environment of the British Isles*, Clarendon Press, 1994.

SIMMONS, I. G. *The Environmental Impact of Later Mesolithic Cultures*, Edinburgh University Press, 1996.

STEPHENS, J. V. et al *Geology of the Country between Bradford and Skipton*, HMSO 1953.

STRAW, A. and CLAYTON, K. M. *Eastern and Central England*, Methuen, 1979.

VERSEY, H. C. *Geology and Scenery of the Countryside round Leeds and Bradford*, Thomas Murby, 1948.

Places to Visit

SHORT TOURS

1. **Allerton Bywater to Woodlesford.** To examine the effects of people on landforms.
2. **Chellow Dene, Bradford to Glovershaw Farm (east of Eldwick).** (Meltwater channels; end moraine and lake flat; glacial diversion of drainage, benches; waterfall).
3. **Hebden Bridge to Haworth.** (Lumb Falls; 400-520m erosion surface).
4. **Hebden Bridge to Todmorden (via Blackshaw Head).** (Benches; tor at Great Bridestones; meltwater channels south west and north west of Todmorden).
5. **Pudsey area:** Duckett's Crossing to Post Hill (via Carr Beck, Pudsey Beck and Farnley Beck). (Meltwater channel; river cliffs; abandoned meanders; west facing escarpments).

FROM THE FIRST FARMER TO THE LAST CONQUEROR

HISTORY IS A contemporary interpretation of the past. Even with sound evidence there can be no definitive history, but when the evidence is sparse, and its meaning obscure, any interpretation must be deemed to be highly uncertain. Such is the case in West Yorkshire in prehistoric, Roman and sub-Roman times, and should be borne in mind when reading the following narrative.

3500 BC TO AD 410

People began to farm in West Yorkshire about 3500 BC, and as farming developed, hunting and gathering came to be mere supplements of the food supply. Farming was a revolutionary change because it brought a more assured supply of food, it eventually enabled settlements to remain in fixed locations for long periods of time and it transformed the landscape.

The first generations to be farmers are known as Neolithic people because they continued the Mesolithic practice of using stone tools. But what tools! Neolithic axes, some of which had been made in Cumbria, were polished and potent, equally capable of felling enemies and trees. With these axes, much woodland was felled, but initially the clearances would have been temporary, if, as seems likely, Early Neolithic people were shifting cultivators. Patches of woodland would be cleared for a year or two and crops, including cereals, would be grown. The cultivated plot would then be abandoned to eventually allow trees to re-grow and soil fertility to recover. The later introduction of manuring, and of leaving an area fallow, enabled cleared areas and settlements to last for longer. In the eastern lowlands, Neolithic people seem to have lived in camps, but the existence of a large Neolithic henge monument at Ferrybridge seems to indicate permanent settlement in its vicinity. In the Pennines, Late Neolithic settlement has been identified at Castle Hill (Almondbury) and probably at Holdsworth (north of Halifax) and Castle Hill (near Denby Dale). As well as growing crops, Neolithic people, particularly in the Pennines, raised domesticated livestock, and continued to hunt wild animals and to gather fruit.

Some 4000 years ago, bronze tools began to replace stone implements, but the extent to which farming and settlement changed is unclear. Just when temporary woodland clearances gave way to much longer lasting, manured fields, is not known. It might have been as early as Late Neolithic times, or as late as the Early Iron Age. Similarly, it is not known if the Early Bronze Age round houses at South Elmsall and Swillington Common represent a new Bronze Age feature or whether such settlements had existed in Late Neolithic times. Nor is it entirely certain if there were far more woodland clearances made in the Early Bronze Age than in the Neolithic, but this seems likely as West Yorkshire is blessed with a relative abundance of Bronze Age remains. Many occur on the moors south of Ilkley and include burial mounds, patterns carved in rock, and stone circles. On Burley Moor, loose boulders have been heaped to form an approximately circular cairn some twenty five metres in diameter and aptly named as Great Skirtful of Stones. Particularly impressive is the stone circle known as Twelve Apostles. This monument is actually slightly oval, with one axis about seventeen metres and another about fourteen metres, and comprises upstanding stone blocks about a metre high (Figure 3.1). The former purpose of these monuments is not known.

Figure 3.1. Twelve Apostles, Burley Moor.

The Early Bronze Age climate was warmer than that of today, so farming probably flourished and population size increased. Organic material can be radiocarbon dated. Compared to earlier and later periods, very few radiocarbon dates for the Late Bronze Age have been found, not only in West Yorkshire but in other parts of northern England. This seems to indicate that population declined in the Late Bronze Age. If this was the case, then it might have been caused by a change to a cooler and wetter climate than that of Neolithic or Early Bronze Age times.

Bronze tools gave way to iron about 700 BC. Throughout West Yorkshire, the Iron Age climate was cool and wet, but the highest parts of the Pennines were cooler and wetter than other parts of the county. Consequently, few, if any, people inhabited the highest parts of the Pennines which were, at best rough grazing land. Elsewhere, there was renewed population growth which was so substantial that woodland was cleared at an alarming rate. Excluding the higher Pennines, and unused floodplains, the landscape acquired a broadly similar appearance throughout the county. Set amongst patches of woodland were small settlements and rectangular fields some of which grew grass and others grew cereals. An individual settlement consisted of one or two houses, each of which had a circular shallow stone base surmounted by a long, tapered, thatched roof. By at least the Early Iron Age, settlements had begun to be enclosed, though probably by no more than palisades. Oldfield Hill (near Meltham) was a Late Iron Age settlement enclosed by a ditch and bank. An ill-defined, approximately one metre deep, ditch and bank enclosure in Gipton Wood, Leeds, is one of several West Yorkshire ditch enclosures that are of uncertain date, but could be Iron Age. The bank and ditch at Oldfield Hill are unlikely to have offered a serious deterrent to tribal attack, but they may have offered a measure of security against thieves. Many ditches and banks were probably designed to prevent livestock from straying and reduce the risk of wolves preying upon livestock. A ditch and bank at Royd Edge, near Oldfield Hill, were primarily used for penning livestock.

One of the wonders of prehistoric West Yorkshire must have been a ditch running some seven kilometres from Cock Beck to Swillington in east Leeds. When freshly dug, the ditch was steep sided, had a narrow flat floor and was about two metres deep. Running alongside the ditch was a bank made from earth thrown up as the ditch was dug. Large parts of Grim's Ditch, as it is now known, have been lost to the plough and to buildings. Even where the earthwork remains, most of it has been infilled, so usually no more than the bank and a shallow ditch are visible (Figure 3.2). Until very recently, both Grim's Ditch and Becca Banks (near Aberford) were believed to be sub-Roman defensive earthworks (chapter eleven). Both are now thought to date from the Iron Age, and Grim's Ditch is now interpreted primarily as a territorial boundary, although a defensive function cannot be completely ruled out.

Romans conquered south east England in AD 43, but it would be some years later before they began to build roads, including the Roman Ridge east of Garforth, and forts in West Yorkshire. Forts were established at Castleford, Ilkley and Slack; these probably became small trading centres supplying the needs of the Roman Garrisons. Although there were no

Figure 3.2. *Grim's Ditch, near Colton, Leeds.* Trevor Plows.

truly urban settlements, small foci may have existed at Bradford, Leeds and Wetherby. In the countryside, some fields were re-organised and made larger. In the eastern lowlands, the area under crops probably increased, and there may have been further woodland clearance. Despite these changes, the landscapes were substantially similar to those of the Iron Age. The highest parts of the Pennines were moorland, used for livestock grazing; the remainder of West Yorkshire was a mosaic of woodland, cropland, grassland, very small clusters of British settlements and a few Roman villas and forts. Perhaps more woodland remained in central West Yorkshire than elsewhere, but even if this were so, prehistoric people had still made a major contribution to the making of the West Yorkshire landscape through their clearance of substantial amounts of woodland.

MOORLAND

Moorland probably owes its existence to prehistoric people, but there is no consensus about the detail suggested below.

By 6000 BC, most of the Pennines was covered by a forest consisting of oak, alder, birch, hazel and very small patches of open land. Later Mesolithic people burnt clumps of trees, and thereby extended the area of open land. However, in a study of Soyland Moor, C.T. Williams did not find any direct evidence of fire at that locality. On the gently sloping summits, Neolithic and Bronze Age people then felled so many trees that the plant communities had become predominantly either grass or heather by the Late Bronze Age.

By then, thick peat growth, which itself was probably a result of human activity, and the possible Late Bronze Age climatic deterioration had made it difficult for forests to re-establish. Since then, moorland has persisted because widespread tree growth has been prevented by livestock trampling infant trees or nibbling at their leaves. Deliberate burning certainly played a key role in developing and maintaining heather communities during the nineteenth and twentieth centuries, but how far regular and controlled burning occurred between Iron Age times and the nineteenth century is uncertain. In some places, perhaps on the less exposed moorland margins, trees re-colonised moorland during sub-Roman times. Thereafter, moorland margins have waxed and waned as reclaimed land has been abandoned or again taken in.

Little is known about the origin of lowland moors. It seems likely that these were also formed by prehistoric people who, in some localities, grew crops to such an extent that the soil lost much of its structure and nutrients. These cultivated areas then had to be given over to livestock grazing which, in turn, prevented widespread tree growth. Eventually, most of these lowland moors were again reclaimed for cultivation, particularly following parliamentary enclosure (chapter four), but a few lowland commons remain as at Heath Common, to the east of Wakefield.

PLACE-NAMES

Place-names are seen so frequently along roads and at railway stations, that they hardly register a thought, yet they possess interesting origins (Figure 3.3). The name Shepley has two elements: shep and ley. Many other places have two elements, but a few, including Shelf, have only one. The elements derive from the languages of the various groups of people who have lived in West Yorkshire. Chevin is probably from Old Welsh, a language spoken by the British who inhabited West Yorkshire at the time of the Roman invasion. Shepley is derived from Old English, a language associated with the Anglo-Saxons, and Micklethwaite's elements are from Old Norse spoken by Scandinavian settlers. A few place-names have a French origin,

Figure 3.3. *Anglo-Saxon Shepley and Scandinavian Micklethwaite.*

one example being Roundhay. The -ley suffix means either a clearing in a wood or a wood, and as shep- means sheep, Shepley is interpreted as a woodland clearing where sheep grazed. Chevin is probably a place under a ridge, Micklethwaite is interpreted as Mickle- (great) and -thwaite (clearing), and Roundhay 'as the round hunting-enclosure.' A personal name often forms a prefix, so Collingham is Cola's folk homestead, and this is another Old English place-name.

Occasionally place-names combine two different languages (Figure 3.4). Examples include Cumberworth, which is derived from the Old Welsh personal name Cumbra and the Old English -worth meaning a valley, and Dewsbury which is Old Welsh personal name Dewi and Old English -bury, a fortification.

Figure 3.4. Cumberworth Church named on the church notice board.

Whilst the majority of settlement names are of ancient origin, large numbers of street names are recent. Bradford has a few ancient street names such as Ivegate and Westgate, the suffix: gate being Old Norse for a road or a street. Nineteenth century street names in Bradford include Gladstone Street, Prospect Terrace, Tennyson Place and Victoria Road. Twentieth century names include Acacia Drive, Loweswater Avenue and Kingfisher Grove.

Place-name interpretation may seem straightforward, but often it is beset with difficulties. A handful have inconclusive interpretations. Halifax is one such name, and whilst the more romantic will prefer "holy hair," the more prosaic will opt for "an area of coarse grass … amongst rocks." More crucially, for the reconstruction of past landscapes from place-names, some suffixes have equally acceptable alternative meanings. As the suffix -ley can mean either a wood or a woodland clearing, little can be ascertained about the degree to which an area was wooded. Similarly the suffix: -ton may mean an enclosure, a farmstead, a village, so -ton provides no evidence about the pattern of settlement. Furthermore, interpretations have changed recently. The view that different Anglo-Saxon suffixes indicate different settlement phases is now considered to be unlikely. The Scandinavian suffix -by is no longer believed to necessarily indicate a pioneer settlement, and in the case of Denby Dale, it almost certainly does not.

AD 410 TO AD 1066

Following the Roman withdrawal, North and East Yorkshire began to be colonised by Anglo-Saxons, but it would be almost two hundred years before the Anglo-Saxons claimed West Yorkshire. Until then (in AD 617), West Yorkshire was part of the Kingdom of Elmet and inhabited by Iron Age descendants. Today, Eccleshill is a Bradford suburb. From its name, Eccleshill seems to have been within the Kingdom of Elmet and to have possessed a church. If this place-name interpretation is correct, then Elmet was a Christian Kingdom. Less certain, but still likely, is that the land of Elmet was held in multiple estates. These are thought to have been very large areas of land which each included different types of land use. The contrasting regions, of a given estate, would have a measure of self-sufficiency, but would also specialise in certain commodities such as animals in the

Pennines and grain in the eastern lowlands, and these specialities would be exchanged between different parts of the estate.

There is a great deal of uncertainty whether population size and the cleared areas were at least maintained, or whether both declined, in the two centuries following the Roman withdrawal. Farms were abandoned and population declined near Hadrian's Wall (on the English-Scottish border) and on the North York Moors, but at some sites in the south of England population and a high level of farming intensity were at least maintained after AD 410. In West Yorkshire, evidence is equally scant for either decline or continuity. At Dalton Parlours (near Collingham), the former Roman villa seems to have been unoccupied (except possibly in Anglo-Saxon times) until the nineteenth century, whereas a recent archaeological excavation at Parlington Hollins, near Garforth, found burials and evidence for buildings that are strongly indicative of post-Roman occupancy at the site.

The issue of continuity or decline is significant as it impinges upon the relative importance of the Anglo-Saxons in clearing woodland in West Yorkshire. If sub-Roman continuity of people and landscape occurred throughout West Yorkshire, it follows that the Anglo-Saxons, who colonised Elmet after AD 617, cleared less woodland and created fewer pioneer settlements than has previously been supposed from the widespread occurrence of place names with -ley suffixes in the central region. However, if substantial decline occurred between 410 and 617, the Anglo-Saxons probably played an important role in the re-clearance and re-settlement of large parts of West Yorkshire. Even if this is the case, many historians no longer believe that the Anglo-Saxons brought the open field type of farming to West Yorkshire or founded villages there. Rather, they resembled the British in living in scattered farmsteads set amongst an enclosed landscape. One of the difficulties in assessing the role of Anglo-Saxons in landscape change, is the reliance that has to be placed on place-name evidence. Only a few Anglo-Saxon artefacts have been found, and of these, fewer still are landscape features. Walton Cross, which stands in a field near Cleckheaton, is believed to mark an Anglo-Saxon cemetery in a now lost settlement (Figure 3.5). One significant change that may be attributed to the Anglo-Saxons is the sub-division of multiple estates into smaller units that either were, or resembled, townships. For example, in the tenth century, there seems to have been a large multiple estate centred upon Otley, and the West Yorkshire part of the estate was divided into townships that included Addingham, Burley, Guiseley, Ilkley and Otley. Four eleventh century major foci of multiple estates have been identified as Kippax, Otley, Tanshelf and Wakefield.

Despite fresh Anglo-Saxon woodland clearances in some places, there is a likelihood that the landscapes of West Yorkshire at the time of Scandinavian colonisation (ninth or tenth centuries) closely resembled those of the Iron Age. Micklethwaite was probably a Scandinavian pioneer settlement, but the numerous Scandinavian place-names in the east are more likely to result from a re-naming of existing settlements rather than to be new creations. It seems almost

Figure 3.5. Walton Cross.

certain that at some time between 900 and 1300 West Yorkshire's landscape was radically transformed into a patchwork of open fields centred upon villages. The most likely periods for this change are those of either the Scandinavian colonisation or the Norman invasion. Unfortunately, West Yorkshire has no evidence that would support one alternative rather than the other. If the first alternative is true, then the Scandinavian settlement had a major impact on the landscape of West Yorkshire; if the second alternative is true, pride of place must go to the Norman invaders.

Places to Visit

Ilkley to examine, on the moors to the south, stone carvings, Twelve Apostles and Great Skirtful of Stones. A cross can be observed in the Parish Church.

Anglo-Saxon crosses may be examined inside **Otley** church or **Walton Cross** may be observed in the open near Cleckheaton.

The Tolson Memorial Museum, Huddersfield, has a display illustrating changes from prehistoric times onwards which affected Huddersfield and district.

Some Sources and Further Reading

DARK, K. R. *External Contacts and the Economy of Late Roman and Post-Roman Britain,* The Boydell Press, 1996.

DEPT. OF PLANNING *Ancient Monuments in Leeds,* Leeds City Council, n/d.

FAULL, M. L. and MOORHOUSE, S. A. *West Yorkshire An Archaeological Survey To AD 1500 Volumes 1 to 4,* West Yorkshire Metropolitan County Council, 1981.

JAMES, E. *Britain In The First Millennium,* Arnold, 2001.

MUIR, R. *The Yorkshire Countryside A Landscape History,* Keele University Press, 1997.

ROBERTS, I., BURGESS, A. and BERG, D. *A New Link to the Past,* West Yorkshire Archaeology Service, 2001.

SMITH, A. H. *The Place-Names Of The West Riding Of Yorkshire, Parts I to VIII,* Cambridge, 1961.

WOOD, P. *A Guide To The Landscape Of Otley Seventh To Seventeenth Century,* Christine Dean and Paul Wood, 1999.

A CHRONOLOGICAL HISTORY OF RURAL LAND USE FROM MEDIEVAL TIMES TO THE MID-TWENTIETH CENTURY

1066 TO 1500

DUKE WILLIAM OF Normandy invaded England in 1066, won a decisive battle and declared himself King of England. Yorkshire folk rebelled against his rule and so, in 1069-70, William led his army to Yorkshire where they slaughtered many people, and laid large areas of countryside to waste. Survivors had often to begin the re-colonisation of farm land, therefore, much of the human landscape of West Yorkshire has a medieval foundation.

OPEN FIELD FARMING AND THE FORMATION OF VILLAGES

By the end of the thirteenth century, open field (or common field) farming had become established throughout the arable land of West Yorkshire. Open field farming varied from one part of West Yorkshire to another, but the type found, by the early fourteenth century, at Hemsworth shows many features that would have been seen in other parts of the county. Hemsworth had three large approximately equal sized arable fields known as north field, east field and south field. Each year one of the three fields was left in fallow, as this enabled soil fertility to be rebuilt after crop growth. Within each field, the land was divided into unenclosed strips hence the term: open field. One Hemsworth married couple, in 1331, owned three acres of land that was made up of nine scattered strips. Slightly away from the three fields were areas of unenclosed moor used for livestock grazing, and woodland to provide fuel wood and building

timber. Gardens were an important source of food in medieval times, and in linear villages, such as Thorner, the crofts (or gardens) formed a row immediately behind each house (Figure 4.1). The most distinctive features of open field farming were the

Figure 4.1. Diagram illustrating the distribution of land use near a medieval village.

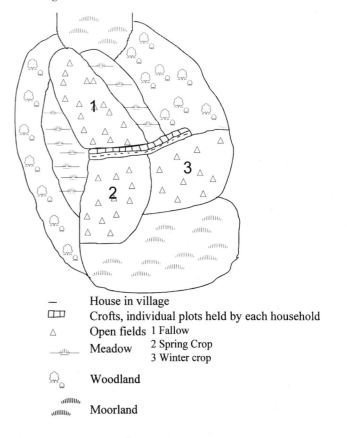

—	House in village
⊞	Crofts, individual plots held by each household
△	Open fields 1 Fallow
	2 Spring Crop
	3 Winter crop
♧	Woodland
⠁⠇⠇	Moorland

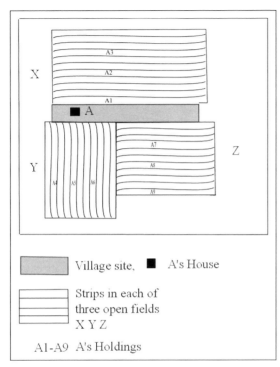

Figure 4.2. Diagram of open field strips.

There is a high level of uncertainty concerning the origin of open field farming and villages, but it does seem likely that the two features are linked. Under open field farming, advantages accrue when people live in villages rather than scattered houses. Ploughing was a co-operative activity, and decisions on land use were taken by the community. These decisions were easier to make when those involved lived near each other. More crucially, for a given farmer, the distance taken to reach his/her scattered strips was minimised by locating the farmhouse in the zone where the three fields were closest to each other (Figure 4.2). But this was equally true of all the other farmers in the township, so their houses were built together thereby creating a village.

ASSARTING

The medieval term for clearing land, particularly woodland, for farming was 'assarting', and in West Yorkshire assarted land was often called 'royd'. Assarting was widespread in the early fourteenth century when the previous two centuries growth in population had come to necessitate extra land to feed hungry bodies. Perhaps assarting was also a means of meeting the needs of individuals of initiative who felt stifled by the communal practices of open field farming. Assarting was undertaken by an individual who, if he was acting legally, paid a fine to the lord of the manor for encroaching upon common waste. Reclamation was very much a piecemeal process, as is evident from an example located at Longley (near Holmfirth) where Matthew de Longley assarted three acres in 1307, one and a half acres a year later, two and a half acres in 1311 and then another three acres in 1315.

This piecemeal clearance, undertaken without prior planning on a map, perhaps led to irregular shaped fields of different sizes. It was a legal requirement that an assart had to

strips, which usually had a reversed S shape, and the unconsolidated individual land holdings (Figure 4.2). Medieval ploughing methods probably account for the reversed S shape of the strips. A team of oxen was needed to pull the heavy ploughs of medieval times. The oxen could be turned only gradually at the end of a field, so the plough, as it followed the oxen, produced a curved end to the strip. Scattered holdings could have originated from a community's desire to ensure that each land holder had equal amounts of good and poor land.

be enclosed and, in West Yorkshire, this was achieved by digging a ditch and/or planting a hedge. Assarting occurred in the eastern lowlands, and gave rise to 'closes' near open fields. However, it was in those intermediate lands, between the high moors and the eastern lowlands, that assarting was particularly prevalent. These lands were well suited to livestock farming, but cereals also had to be grown in the medieval subsistence economy, so enclosure helped prevent livestock from straying over crops. Enclosure also had the advantage of reducing the risk of livestock being attacked by predators.

New settlements developed on those assarted lands that were some distance from a village. But these new settlements were built by people who sought to minimise the distance taken to reach their individually held fields, and so a pattern of scattered farmhouses developed rather than villages. Such a settlement pattern is called dispersed, whereas a series of villages forms a nucleated pattern.

During the mid-fourteenth century, the Black Death intensified a decline in population size which had already commenced in West Yorkshire. Moorland re-advanced in those places where assarts were abandoned, and widespread colonisation of the land would not recommence until the sixteenth century.

THE ROLE OF THE MONASTERIES

Monks played an important part in the economy of medieval West Yorkshire because of the large amounts of West Yorkshire land held by abbeys and priories including the abbeys of Byland and Rievaulx located in North Yorkshire. Secular land owners awarded gifts of land to monasteries, but as abbeys and priories received far more gifts than nunneries, it was monks, rather than nuns, who had the greater impact on the landscape.

Monasteries held land throughout West Yorkshire. At East Keswick – located in the eastern lowlands, which were already recovering from the harrying of the north by the time many monasteries were established – monks merely collected rent from their property. However, in the Pennines, the effect of the monasteries was far greater as monks were responsible for the reclamation of parts of the waste. A grange (house) was built to be occupied by a lay brother who organised the running of a farm. The monks of Kirkstall had numerous becaries (sheep farms) including Allerton Grange and Moor Grange, and owned, in total, some 4500 sheep. Byland Abbey held a sheep farm as far away as White Cross at Emley. Monks also established vaccaries (cattle farms), and promoted mining activities in several areas, one of which was the Emley district.

Part of the Tankersley Ironstone bed runs from Thornhill, through Flockton and Emley to West Bretton. It is not known when this ironstone was first worked, but it is known that various abbeys were involved in its exploitation. Rievaulx Abbey worked the ore at Flockton, Middlestown and Overton, and Byland Abbey extracted that at Emley, Midgley (near Emley) and West Bretton. At Emley, Bentley Grange was the main centre of the industry, and the farm there provided food for its iron ore workers. Wood from nearby places such as Furnace Hill was used to smelt the iron ore either at Furnace Grange or White Cross.

The sixteenth century dissolution of the monasteries did not bring iron ore mining to an end; at Emley, for example, mining continued until the eighteenth century (Figure 4.3). It was also the monks of Byland Abbey who began to mine coal near Flockton. Throughout the Pennines, small quantities of coal were mined by monks or others, from medieval times to the nineteenth century; coal output then substantially increased.

Figure 4.3. Post-medieval iron working, Bentley Grange.

1500 TO 1780

REBUILDING IN STONE

Almost all medieval houses, even those of the gentry, had been constructed of timber, but by 1500 supplies of wood were becoming harder to find. Woodland had been cleared by assarting, and trees had been felled to make charcoal for the smelting industries. The gentry began to encase their timber framed houses in stone, wholly as at Old Hall, Calverley, partially as at Lees Hall, Thornhill. Little is known about houses of poorer people, but houses of the yeomen are well represented. Many are evident in upper Calderdale, particularly at Sowerby Bridge and from there northwards up Luddenden Dean and southwards into Norland. No two yeomen houses are exactly alike, but they are characterised by mullioned windows. In upper Calderdale the houses are often large (Figure 4.4). Rebuilding in stone began towards the end of the sixteenth century in upper Calderdale, which was rather earlier than in other parts of West Yorkshire. Timber was used for rebuilding in the eastern lowlands until the late seventeenth century, and yeomen houses were often smaller than those in upper Calderdale. Houses built of stone were more expensive than those of timber, so the earlier rebuilding in, and the larger houses of, upper Calderdale reflect the area's greater wealth in the seventeenth century. A combination of farming and textile manufacture had contributed to upper Calderdale's great wealth. As more and more buildings were made of stone, so stone quarrying increased, particularly in the Pennines which became pockmarked with quarries.

Figure 4.4. Lower Old Hall, Norland

POPULATION GROWS

The mid-fourteenth century decline in population had been reversed by the sixteenth century when there was renewed population growth. This stimulated further encroachment upon the waste. Reclamation was piecemeal, but widespread, in the Pennine valleys. Farmers decided to minimise the distance to reach their fields by building a farmhouse on their new holding rather than remain in a parent village. By the late eighteenth century, the village of Old Oxenhope had all but disappeared by this process, and, complementary to this change, a line of new farmhouses developed from North Ives to Mouldgreave.

The second half of the seventeenth century was a period of fluctuating population size with little or no growth, but by the early eighteenth century, there was renewed population growth which largely continued to the First World War. Within the Pennines, a holding was equally divided amongst the children when their parents died. At a time of population growth, this led to many small holdings that were only made viable by extra income derived from textile manufacture. A new house might be built on the more distant divided holding or a new house could be built in the farm yard of an existing house (Figure 4.5). This process produced many of the small clusters of two or three houses that were even then a characteristic component of Pennine settlement.

Many villages continued to exist, and at least three new ones were created. Fulneck was founded in 1748 by the Moravian Church. Gildersome and Liversedge, which had probably begun as individual settlements linked to assarts, had grown into villages by the eighteenth century. The settlement pattern remained predominantly nucleated in the eastern lowlands. Although some medieval villages, including Potterton and Wothersome, had been lost, Boston Spa had originated, in 1753, to exploit its mineral waters.

Between 1500 and 1780 farming had changed in all parts of West Yorkshire, but the greatest changes had probably taken place in the Pennines. Although some cereals, mainly oats, were still being grown, the area under grass had increased as it was used not only to feed livestock, but to hold tenter frames on which cloth dried. The days of a subsistence economy were well gone: the sale of woollen cloth enabled people to buy food from other parts of Yorkshire and from Lancashire, Lincolnshire and Nottinghamshire. Open fields, if they existed at all, were few indeed. In the eastern lowlands, the number of "closes" had increased since 1500 at the expense of waste, woodland and open field. Nevertheless, large areas of land remained open field.

Figure 4.5. A small cluster of houses at Dry Carr, Luddenden Dean.

1780 TO 1960

PARLIAMENTARY ENCLOSURE

Most of the open fields that still existed in West Yorkshire, in 1780, were soon to be enclosed following Acts of Parliament. Such Acts arose from the land holders of the township petitioning Parliament for the enclosure of the township's open fields and commons. Though each Act was individual, the form was replicated time and again so that one Act is distinguishable from another chiefly by its names.

It was claimed that great benefits to farming would ensue from enclosure, and there was at least partial truth in this assertion. When holdings lay in scattered strips, it was difficult for a farmer with initiative to introduce new husbandry, such as hoeing turnips, if none of his neighbours were to practice in this way. There were other, more hidden, reasons for enclosure in some places. Migrants, many of them Irish, were flowing into Dewsbury to work in the rapidly expanding early nineteenth century textile industry, and to live in new houses built on the moor. In an attempt to prevent further encroachment, the land was enclosed. Ultimately this failed as the enclosed lands were later sold as building plots. Parliamentary enclosure in Keighley and other parts of the Worth valley may have been motivated by the need to secure mineral rights, particularly coal, at a time when steam power was beginning to replace water power. Whether that was the case, the newly enclosed lands in the Worth valley seemed to be no more productive than the previous unenclosed common.

Enclosed waste usually became more productive in the eastern lowlands. It was also in this area that the benefits of enclosure were markedly enhanced by the consolidation of holdings. Consolidation created fields that were somewhat irregular in shape but inclined to that of a square. Large numbers of farmers decided to build a new house set amongst their consolidated holding, but a few farmhouses remained in villages when the farmhouses happened to be near the farmers' fields. Despite the movement of farmers from the village to their new holdings, villages persisted. Houses were occupied by such people as blacksmiths, grocers and workers in rural manufacturing. Thorner, for example, manufactured textiles.

Parliamentary enclosure in the Pennines usually came later than in the eastern lowlands and was virtually restricted to common or waste. The resultant fields had remarkably straight boundaries, as they had been planned on maps before outdoor construction. On Cartworth Moor, which was enclosed in 1832, many field boundaries were orientated at right angles to the roads (Figure 4.6). Some fields were almost square shaped, but

Figure 4.6. A pattern of fields and roads derived from parliamentary enclosure, Cartworth Moor (south west of Holmfirth).

many were rectangular, and these patterns, with some parallelograms, occurred throughout the areas of parliamentary enclosure. The size of the fields varied, but many were small. Roads were often wide and they were certainly straight because the roads, like the fields, had been planned (Figure 4.6). Some roads, such as Issues Road (north west of Holme), led nowhere as they were merely built to enable farmers to reach their new holdings. When someone acquired a viable holding, a house was often built within the holding, and frequently this was a laithe house. A laithe combines in one building a cow house and a barn, and a laithe house is one with the laithe attached to the house (Figure 4.7). Laithe houses were well suited to a small holder, as a combined building was cheaper to build than separate buildings, and, when built, were partially warmed by heat generated from livestock in the laithe. Large numbers of laithe houses were built, and added yet another feature to the already varied Pennine settlement pattern.

Figure 4.7. Elysium, a laithe house in the former township of Cartworth.

CHANGES IN FARMING

Messrs Rennie, Broun and Shirreff compiled a fascinating report on West Riding agriculture in 1799. They describe a pattern not unfamiliar to that of today. The higher moorlands were grazed by sheep; the lower Pennines were mostly in grass, but with small areas of corn, and near the towns, manufacturer's kept dairy cattle for their own use. In the eastern lowlands, crops predominated, with the highest proportion of arable to be found in the south eastern corner. Specialities had emerged near Pontefract where liquorice and rhubarb were both grown, but much of the eastern arable still included large areas of fallow, and was otherwise dominated by cereals, especially wheat and oats. Some farmers had replaced fallow with turnips or grass, but the hoeing of turnips had commenced only twenty years previously, and was still an uncommon sight. Enclosure and the consolidation of holdings enabled farmers to modernise, but there was no compulsion to adopt the new husbandry, and, at East Keswick, tenant farmers could opt for either the old or the new rotation until at least 1858.

The Napoleonic Wars stimulated an increase in the area under cereals in both the Pennines and the eastern lowlands. Cereals, especially wheat, continued to be very important in the east until about 1870. However, after 1870 increasing amounts of cheaply grown wheat, cheaply transported by steam ships, were imported from North America, and so the price of wheat slumped in Britain. Consequently, the area growing wheat declined sharply in West Yorkshire, and some crop land was put down to grass in the eastern lowlands. Grass also increased in the Pennines, and commercial dairying became the main activity on a large number of farms.

Perhaps the greatest change in the second half of the nineteenth century was the expansion of market gardening, located particularly on the margins of Leeds and Wakefield. Whilst vegetables were grown, the most distinctive product was rhubarb. The whole of West Yorkshire has the advantage of cool autumns which allow rhubarb a dormant spell before it is transferred to forcing sheds where early, high value rhubarb is grown (Figure 9.9). A combination of advantages helped to concentrate the growth of rhubarb within a Bradford-Leeds-Wakefield triangle. Woollen mills provided shoddy which was added to the soil to help release the nitrogen required for rhubarb growth. Numerous coal mines in the area provided the cheap coal used to heat the forcing sheds. As rhubarb is a crop that gives high returns from a small area, it was suited to small sized farms that occurred on high value land near towns. Leeds and Bradford provided large nearby markets, but there was also a nation-wide market. The then recently built railway lines enabled distant markets, such as London, to be quickly reached.

Towards the end of the First World War, food shortages led to the ploughing up of some of the eastern grasslands and an increase in wheat growth. But this was a short-lived phase, and, in the 1920s, arable farmers again fell on hard times, and some land reverted to grass. By the thirties central government intervened and set up marketing boards for milk, and introduced subsidies and import quotas to assist arable farmers. At the outbreak of the Second World War, in 1939, farming had begun to improve, but sixty per cent. of our foodstuffs were still imported. Yet again, the government initiated a ploughing up campaign, and throughout West Yorkshire some grass was ploughed up and replaced by cereals. After the war, central government decided that never again would we be so perilously dependent upon food imports, and so marketing boards and subsidies continued to, and beyond, the 1960s. Whilst some of the ploughed up Pennine fields reverted to grass, in the eastern lowlands large areas remained under crops especially cereals. The area under wheat and barley increased at the expense of oats. The latter crop had been chiefly used to feed horses so the demand for oats plummeted when horses were replaced by motor vehicles and motorised ploughs and harvesters. These ploughs and harvesters are most cost effective when used in large fields hence, after the war, many hedges between fields were uprooted making way for larger fields.

The rapidly growing urban populations of the nineteenth century and the large number of twentieth century urban dwellers created an increased demand for water which was met by building sixty reservoirs in the Pennines prior to 1960. Many reservoirs were built in, or near, moorland areas as population was so sparse in these areas that few, if any, people had to be re-settled when a chosen site went under water. Also, moorland areas are amongst the wettest in West Yorkshire, so there is less risk that reservoirs will completely empty through insufficient rain. Each large town built its own set of reservoirs. Huddersfield, for example, opened a nearby reservoir at Longwood as early as 1828, but by 1954 had moved further afield to Digley. Wakefield built a number of reservoirs in the Rishworth area including Ringstone (1888) and Baitings (1957), (Figure 9.11).

KING COAL

During the nineteenth century, the demand for coal soared as the number of steam powered mills increased, and as vast numbers of new houses with coal fires were built. Old shallow workings proved totally incapable of meeting the increased demand for coal. As a result, deep mines opened, and new landscapes of sporadic pit head winding gear with adjacent spoil heaps and substantial railway sidings developed.

Between 1870 and 1914 many new mines opened in the eastern lowlands, but coal mining declined in the Pennines. During the nineteenth century, open cast coal mining had taken place on a limited scale. However, it was not until the Second World War brought a huge increase in the demand for coal, that large scale open cast mining commenced in 1942. Coal mining was nationalised in 1947, and by then, mining was concentrated in the east. The National Coal Board improved deep mines that still had potential, but began to close those which had low reserves or high production costs. Open cast coal mining has continued to the present day because mining costs are relatively low. In addition, in the immediate post-war period, any environmental concern was outweighed by the great demand for coal. Today, the deep mining of coal has effectively ended in West Yorkshire, and it seems that open cast mining could soon go the same way.

Open cast mining has been concentrated in those rural parts of the eastern lowlands that lie to the south and south west of Barnbow. The landscape is greatly disturbed by open cast workings, but, at any given site, working is usually short-lived, and areas mined prior to the mid-sixties have been reclaimed. Quite often, these former open cast sites are not immediately obvious in the landscape.

In those areas where coal was deep mined, existing villages, such as Upton, were altered by the need to accommodate large numbers of miners, whilst the villages of Fitzwilliam and New Micklefield were solely established to house miners working in nearby collieries. Before the commencement of coal mining, in 1926, Upton was a linear village. With the building of large numbers of miner's houses, Upton acquired two comparatively compact cores and a size commensurate with that of a small town, but without urban functions. By 1926,

(a)    (b)

Figure 4.8. Contrasts in miners' houses. (a) New Micklefield c.1910. Marjorie Plows collection. *(b) Upton, inter-war houses as they appeared in 2001.*

workers houses were being built to a higher standard than prior to 1914, hence the landscape of Upton differs from the older brick terraces of Fitzwilliam or the stone terraces of New Micklefield (Figure 4.8).

From 1800 coal was by far the most important mineral to be mined in West Yorkshire, but some iron ore was worked, especially near Bradford at such places as Low Moor and Bowling. The iron ore mined was the Black Bed ironstone found within the Coal Measures. Somewhat surprisingly, stone was also mined: the Elland flagstones were mined in a zone between Halifax and Bramley. Nevertheless, most stone was extracted from surface quarries and the industry reached its peak during the nineteenth century. Stone was quarried to enclose fields, to build the new laithe houses, and to meet the vastly increased demand for stone built mills and workers' houses in Bradford, Halifax, Huddersfield and Keighley. The market for stone was more than local, and Bramley Fall stone was used as far away as London.

Places to Visit

Cartworth Moor. To observe a parliamentary enclosure landscape including laithe houses.

Clifton. Probable traces of open fields.

Digley Reservoir (west of Holmfirth).

Emley. Old mineral workings; monastic granges; Emley Cross and parliamentary enclosure of Emley Moor.

Fitzwilliam, New Micklefield and Upton. Contrasting mining villages.

Luddenden Dean. Yeomen's houses; dispersed settlement pattern.

National Coal Mining Museum Caphouse Colliery (west of Wakefield).

Some Sources and Further Reading

BAUMBER, M. L. *A Pennine Community On The Eve Of The Industrial Revolution,* no publisher, n/d.

BAUMBER, M. L. *From Revival to Regency A History of Keighley and Haworth 1740-1820,* ML Baumber, 1983.

BROWN, T. W. *The Making of a Yorkshire Village-Thorner,* Thorner and District Historical Society, 1991.

BULLEY, J. A. *Hemsworth In History,* 1959.

COLLUM, G. *Rural Houses Of West Yorkshire 1400-1830,* HMSO, 1986.

FAULL, M. L. and MOORHOUSE, S. A. *West Yorkshire An Archaeological Survey to AD 1500 Volumes 1 to 4,* West Yorkshire Metropolitan County Council, 1981.

GOODCHILD, J. *The Story of Rhubarb* in TAYLOR, K. Aspects of Wakefield, Wharncliffe, 1998.

NO NAMED AUTHOR. *Land At War,* HMSO, 1945 reprinted 2001.

POBJOY, H. N. *A History of Emley,* 1970.

ROWLEY, T. *The Origins of Open Field Agriculture,* Croom Helm, 1981.

TRANSPORT IN THE LANDSCAPE

ROADS, OR AT least trackways, already existed in prehistoric times, yet the road network is still growing today. However, during the eighteenth and nineteenth centuries, the relative significance of roads declined as first the waterway, and then the railway network developed. Today, roads are again the predominant form of transport. The histories of roads, waterways and railways have been so different that each mode of transport must be discussed separately.

ROADS

AD 80 to 1787

The Romans probably established a network of roads that connected each of their forts. To date, only a few stretches of road have been definitely identified as Roman, one of which coincides with a contemporary road between Castleford and Aberford. Roman Roads were straight, broad and paved, whereas most medieval roads were little more than ill-defined, earthen tracks. Better surfaced roads were scarcely warranted when traffic flows were as low as in the subsistence economy of medieval times. Nevertheless, some localised but essential goods, such as salt, had to be moved from place to place. One saltway from the Cheshire saltfields took a route through Colne to reach Otley and district (Figure 5.1). Bingley was linked to the Otley Road by either Tewitt Lane or Birch Close Lane. The latter was busy when the monks of Rievaulx Abbey held land in Harden, parts of which were used for iron working. Packhorses took advantage of a causeway along Tewitt Lane and, in the eighteenth century, this was followed

by horse riders who included the well-known Methodist John Wesley (Figure 5.2).

The Tewitt Lane causeway is but one of many that still remain in the Pennines. Causeways are slabs of sandstone or gritstone that were laid to provide firm, albeit narrow, foundations for travellers and packhorses. Bridges carrying causeways are just as narrow, for they were built only wide enough for a pony to pass across (Figure 5.3). A number of packhorse bridges can still be seen in the Pennines including those at Crimsworth Dean (Figure 2.2a)), and Close Gate

Figure 5.1. *Selected Highways in the Otley District.*

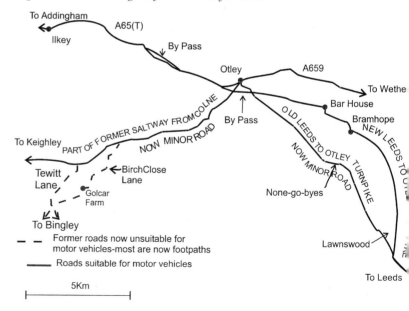

Figure 5.2. *Tewitt Lane with a causeway on the left. Notice the ruts to the right.*

Figure 5.3. *Close Gate Bridge, west of Marsden.*

located two kilometres to the west of Marsden. A bridge that resembles Close Gate, but was built to provide the vicar with a short cut to his church, is located in the village of Marsden.

Many causeways may have been built, in the sixteenth century, to meet the needs of the then expanding woollen textile industry. By the eighteenth century, trade had increased to such an extent that horse waggons, which could carry more goods per horse than packhorses, were growing in popularity. Horse waggons and stagecoaches were too wide for causeways, which meant they had to use road surfaces that became muddy and rutted in wet weather. Dry weather then hardened the ruts which at best presented an uncomfortable ride, at worst brought an increased risk of accidents (Figure 5.2). In an attempt to remedy this situation,

turnpike trusts were established. Trustees were allowed to borrow money to improve roads and to obtain income at turnpikes. These were gates which barred the passage of traffic until any necessary toll had been paid. A toll keeper was needed at each bar, and had to be available twenty four hours a day, so a house was provided. Usually, the house was a single story building with the windows so arranged as to provide a good view of traffic arriving from all directions (Figure 5.4).

Lancashire possessed turnpike roads before any existed in West Yorkshire, and the first West Yorkshire turnpike road to gain approval, in 1735, was one linking Rochdale and Halifax. Many of the proposals, made between 1735 and 1759, to turnpike West Yorkshire's roads gained parliamentary

Figure 5.4. Old Pool Bank toll house. Margaret Plows

1787 to 1920

By 1787 West Yorkshire possessed a well developed road network that bears comparison with the network of today (Figure 5.5). Many of these 1787 roads were turnpike roads, but they were not new roads, they were merely attempts to improve existing roads. However, from about the time Cary was producing his map until 1850, new roads, of which many, but not all, were turnpikes began to be built. An Act to allow the Leeds to Otley turnpike to be diverted was passed in 1837, but the diversion was not opened until 1842. This new road was built between Otley and Lawnswood, and passed through Bramhope (Figure 5.1). East of Lawnswood, the existing turnpike through Headingley continued to be used. The new road was built to provide a much gentler average gradient to the south of Otley than that on the old turnpike. Between Otley and Old Pool Bank toll house, an average gradient of one in thirty five enabled coaches and waggons to move faster, and with some measure of safety, than had been previously possible.

New roads were also built to provide straighter routes between places. The Wakefield to Aberford turnpike (1794) was built to replace a series of "very crooked and indirect roads" between the two places. Straighter still was a new road between Armley and Stanningley which was part of a more direct route between Leeds and Bradford than either the original turnpike via Burley, Kirkstall and Bramley or a later diversion through Bramley along Leeds and Bradford Road. The Armley diversion had only become possible when Wellington Bridge had opened in 1819. Many new local roads were also built between 1787 and 1850. They were planned as straight roads as part of the process of parliamentary enclosure (chapter four).

Between 1850 and 1920 railways were the predominant mode of transport. Apart from the numerous streets built in

approval. One of these roads was the Leeds to Otley turnpike (1755), which was justified on the grounds that the domestic manufacture of woollen textiles had spread to new places. In 1775 this turnpike followed the course of a road that was in existence in 1720 between Leeds and Otley via Woodhouse, Headingley and None Go Byes (Figure 5.1). Consequently, the turnpike inherited a steep gradient of one in nine just to the south of Otley. How far the surface of the road was improved, prior to the nineteenth century, is unknown. Contemporary opinion as to the state of the roads varied. In the late eighteenth century, Arthur Young described the Leeds to Wakefield turnpike as "stony and ill-made" whereas the Rev Thomas Twining was well pleased with his ride along turnpikes in the Calder valley.

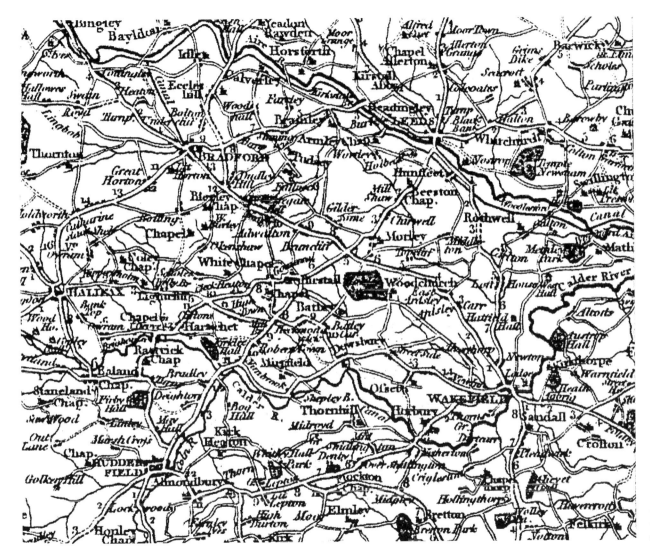

Figure 5.5. Extract from the South Part of the West Riding of Yorkshire, J Cary, 1787.

areas of urban housing, almost no new roads were built. Turnpikes became disturnpiked, but the roads themselves remain in the landscape.

1920 to 2003

From 1920 (except for the war years from 1939-45) motor vehicle usage increased to such an extent that by the 1980s, widespread congestion, especially in towns and cities, ensued. Ring roads and bypasses have been built in an attempt to reduce such actual or foreseen traffic congestion. A wide twentieth century bridge over the Calder at Wakefield carries vehicular traffic, and so bypasses the narrower medieval bridge which has become a footbridge. Each of the bypasses at Otley, Drighlington and Hemsworth partly follows a dismantled railway line, but the Keighley bypass was built at the expense of green fields. The Keighley bypass is part of an Aire Valley Trunk road which is being extended south eastwards to bypass Bingley.

West Yorkshire has two main motorways: the M1 and the M62; the latter was the first to be built in West Yorkshire and opened in 1971. From the M62, there is a branch to the southern edge of Bradford and a branch which almost reaches the centre of Leeds. Motorways avoided town centres because it was too difficult and expensive to construct them through areas that were already densely built up. Both of the main motorways were built to shorten journey times by maintaining a steady flow of vehicles. Unlike early roads, motorways have demanded major engineering works, including cuttings, such as Deanhead, fifty five metres deep, to provide the very gentle gradients that allow vehicles to travel at constant high speeds. A recent addition to the motorway network has been made to the east of Leeds, and, in the north east, the A1 has been upgraded to become the A1(M).

WATERWAYS

Rivers might seem to be an obvious mode of transport, but until the eighteenth century, West Yorkshire's rivers had sections that were not navigable so there was no waterway network. During the eighteenth and early nineteenth centuries, a waterway network developed by making the lower reaches of the Aire and the Calder navigable, and by the building of canals (Figure 5.6).

Figure 5.6. West Yorkshire Waterways at the end of 1849.

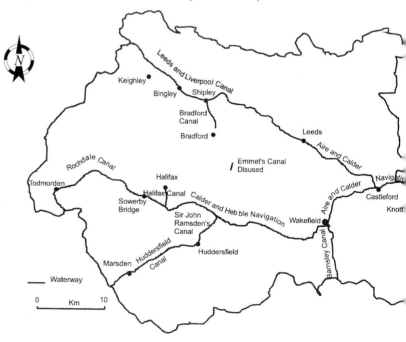

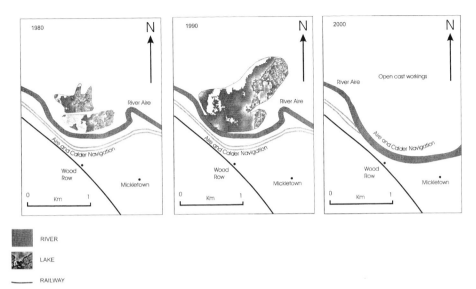

RIVER

LAKE

—— RAILWAY

Figure 5.7. *The Aire and Calder Navigation between Fleet Lock and Woodend.*

The Aire and Calder Navigation, and the Calder and Hebble Navigation

An Act of 1699 allowed the Aire and Calder Navigation Company to make the Aire navigable upstream to Leeds and the Calder upstream to Wakefield. This was achieved by 1704, but further improvements followed, and by 1850 a canal existed alongside the River Aire between Knowsthorpe and Woodend. Today, the valley floor between Fleet Lock and Woodend is most unusual in that the canal has been re-united with the river (Figure 5.7). In 1988 the Aire burst its banks and flooded St Aidan's opencast working creating a much enlarged lake. In order to drain the lake, and to reduce the risk of future flooding, the Aire and the canal were combined and re-located

southwards. Between Woodend and Knottingley cuts are few, and, apart from dredging, the river is little altered from that of 1699.

By the time the Calder and Hebble Navigation opened, in 1770, a number of locks and cuts had made the Calder navigable between Sowerby Bridge and Wakefield. But down valley, between Wakefield and Whitwood, the meandering and shallow Calder would not be substantially improved for navigation until 1839 when a seven kilometre cut was opened. A huge aqueduct had to be constructed to carry the canal over the river near Stanley Ferry; but the aqueduct proved vulnerable to subsidence, and so a new structure opened alongside the old in 1981.

The nature of canals

A broad canal has a narrowest width of 4.25 metres or more, and all the canals in West Yorkshire are broad except for the Huddersfield Narrow Canal (Figure 5.8). The Huddersfield was built as a narrow canal because it was much cheaper to build a narrow five kilometre long tunnel under Standedge than a broad tunnel. Standedge tunnel had to be dug because the Colne valley ends steeply. To minimise building costs, the tunnel was built without a towpath, and boats were propelled by boatmen lying flat on their backs walking against the tunnel roof.

The other two trans-Pennine canals had easier routes into Lancashire: the Leeds and Liverpool Canal followed the Aire Gap, and the Rochdale Canal followed a former meltwater channel. Despite these advantages, both canals, like the

Figure 5.9. *Three rise locks near Kirkstall Forge. On the Leeds and Liverpool Canal locks were often built in rises so as to provide long streches of canal without locks.*

Figure 5.8. *The Huddersfield Narrow Canal near Marsden.*

Huddersfield, required locks to provide the necessary flat stretches (Figure 5.9). Locks were expensive to build, are costly to maintain, and slow the passage of vessels. Were it not for specifically constructed reservoirs, the water level in a canal would fall when barges use locks. Such large quantities of water are needed to replenish canals that two extensive, adjacent reservoirs, at Cold Hiendley and Wintersett, had to be constructed to feed the Barnsley Canal (Figure 5.10). Although the Barnsley Canal was abandoned in 1953, these two large reservoirs remain for their scenic, wildlife and recreational value. Both reservoirs are used by anglers, and Wintersett is valued for sailing. Other West Yorkshire reservoirs which continue to feed the county's canals include the Gaddings, White Holme and Slaithwaite. Canal builders sought to minimise the number of locks, and reduce the

Figure 5.10. Cold Hiendley reservoir in 2003.

number of other engineering works, to keep costs low. As engineering works could be kept to a minimum by locating canals in lowlands or the larger valley floors, so most of the canals of West Yorkshire were located in the Aire, Calder and Colne valleys. Nevertheless, cuttings were needed in some places, particularly on parts of the Barnsley Canal where spurs had to be cut through, as there was no major valley to follow.

In the early years of canal transport, horses towed barges, but at only a slow speed. Towpaths, where horses once toiled, are now followed by cyclists and walkers exercising for pleasure. Barge speeds have always been kept low by the need to reduce wash that might otherwise increase erosion of canal banks, and by the time spent passing through locks.

The canal network

With all the problems of canal transport, it might well be wondered why so many were built in eighteenth century West Yorkshire. Briefly, this was a time when trade was increasing, but alternative modes of transport were poor or scarcely existent. Furthermore, for low value, heavy or bulky goods such as coal and timber, road transport was more expensive than waterways. The promoters of the Leeds and Liverpool Canal perceived its advantages as the distribution of goods imported through Hull and Liverpool and the carriage of limestone and coal. More than any other canal, the Barnsley was built to carry coal, especially the large quantities obtained from Silkstone. Competition and emulation had each a part to play in eighteenth century canal building. It was the success enjoyed by the Bridgewater Canal (in Lancashire) that led Halifax born John Longbotham to propose the building of a canal from Leeds to Liverpool. When it became clear, in 1766, that the proposed Leeds and Liverpool Canal would be routed well away from Manchester, some Rochdale men proposed a rival canal, along the Calder valley, to link the Calder and Hebble with one of the Lancashire canals. Compared to the Leeds and Liverpool, it would be a shorter trans-Pennine crossing and would link Manchester with Hull. For some years little progress was made, and this allowed yet another rival group, of predominantly Ashton Canal shareholders, to promote the Huddersfield Canal which would link two existing canals: the Ashton and Sir John Ramsden's. Both of the proposals gained Parliamentary approval in 1794, but had the Rochdale gained earlier approval, it is doubtful if the Huddersfield, with its more difficult course, would have been built.

Railways offered strong competition to canals from 1840, yet, with the exception of Emmet's Canal which had been closed much earlier (c.1815), no canal was to be abandoned until the Bradford in 1922. The Halifax was abandoned in 1942, the Huddersfield in 1944 and, though not used by commercial traffic since 1937, the Rochdale in 1952. A year later the Barnsley was abandoned, but at the Barnsley end commercial traffic had ceased in 1946, chiefly as a result of subsidence and associated problems of flooding.

Today the Barnsley is really a series of very elongated lakes, parts of which are being choked by plant growth, though former locks partially remain at Walton (near Wakefield). The course of Emmet's Canal is still very evident in the landscape as a gently bending, narrow, grass covered bench of almost constant elevation, fronted, in one section, by a shallow embankment. In sharp contrast, the Bradford Canal might never have existed for its only remains are a couple of bridges

Figure 5.11. Waterbus on the Leeds and Liverpool Canal near Saltaire.

over its former path to the east of Frizinghall railway station. The Aire and Calder Navigation is used to transport petroleum from the Humber estuary to the outskirts of Leeds, otherwise, contemporary West Yorkshire waterways are almost entirely used by pleasure traffic (Figure 5.11). It was this potential traffic, along with the growth in the conservation movement, that led to the re-opening of the Rochdale Canal. The Huddersfield re-opened, in 2001, with the aim of encouraging tourist trade in the Colne valley and, to this end, improvements to the canal landscape have been made at Slaithwaite. As a result of the re-opening of these two canals, the waterway network again closely resembles that which existed at its peak.

RAILWAYS

1745 to 1849
A waggonway (a railway along which horses pulled waggons) existed in 1745 at Outwood. Other waggonways were soon built including one which opened in 1758 to carry coal from Middleton to Leeds. In 1812 this became the first railway in the world both to be worked by a steam locomotive, and to be commercially successful. It is still working today, but now carries people for a pleasure trip rather than coal. Twenty two years elapsed before the Leeds and Selby Railway became West Yorkshire's first public passenger and goods railway. Between 1840 and 1850, railway lines spread rapidly throughout the county to form a network which had developed to connect West Yorkshire with other parts of the country (Figure 5.12). Steam engines could pull trains quickly, only when the tracks had very gentle gradients. Where these did not exist, engineers had to create them by building such features as embankments and cuttings. The fewer the

Figure 5.12. The Railway Network of West Yorkshire at the end of 1849.

1849 to 1914

After 1849 only a few lines, including the Leeds to Harrogate (via Wetherby) and the Wakefield to Doncaster, were built to connect centres within West Yorkshire to those outside the county (Figure 5.13). Nevertheless, the period between 1849 and 1914 witnessed a huge expansion in the railway network of West Yorkshire that was designed to meet demands from within the county.

Many new lines were built to provide shorter alternatives to existing lines. Prior to 1850, it was theoretically possible to travel between Bradford and Manchester by a long circuitous route though Leeds. In practice, people had to be content with a coach to Brighouse where a connection was made with a

Figure 5.13. The former Great Northern mainline, between Wakefield and Doncaster, at South Elmsall. This line did not open until 1866, as earlier attempts to build such a line had been repeatedly thwarted.

engineering works, the lower the building costs. In the Pennines, lower costs were achieved by following, as far as possible, the valley floors of the main rivers. So the first railway to reach Bradford did not take the shortest route from Leeds, but followed the Aire valley north westwards to Shipley and thence southwards along Bradford Beck valley to Bradford. The Manchester and Leeds Railway curved along the Calder valley, and then followed a former meltwater channel between Todmorden and Summit tunnel (Figure 2.5). From Todmorden, a line to Burnley followed another former meltwater channel.

Manchester bound train. When a branch from the Manchester to Leeds railway reached Halifax, Bradford citizens most strongly urged that the line from Halifax should be extended to Bradford. After numerous set-backs, this line, and another line from Low Moor to Mirfield (on the Manchester to Leeds line), were built. Soon after, Bradford achieved further success when it obtained a line to Leeds, via Stanningley, that was shorter than that via the Aire valley.

During the nineteenth century, there were many different railway companies that sometimes competed for traffic. For example, The Great Northern sought to strengthen its foothold in the Batley area, and this led the company to build a line, from the Leeds to Bradford via Stanningley line, to Dudley Hill. Near there, short connecting lines were built which then gave Bradford a third route to Leeds. The London and North Western Railway actually built an alternative set of lines, between Leeds and Huddersfield, to its own existing lines via Dewsbury. This arose because traffic was increasing to such an extent that the two existing lines could not cope, and these lines should have been doubled. Old mine working to the north of Dewsbury made doubling the lines an untenable proposition, so the company built a completely new route via Gomersal.

The mining of coal also created additional railway lines. Bradford's demand for coal led to the building of a line from Laisterdyke to coal mines near Gildersome. Coincidentally, a shorter route between Leeds and Wakefield, via Ardsley, was being built, so it was decided to extend the Laisterdyke to Gildersome line to Ardsley, thereby creating an alternative line between Bradford and Wakefield. Numerous branch lines also owed their origin to coal mining. Many, like the Snydale Junction to Featherstone Main Colliery and to Don Pedro Pit, were solely used to move coal from pits. The Aberford to Garforth line was initially built to carry coal, but also carried passengers between 1837–40 and again from 1852.

Branch lines developed for other sets of reasons. Some were initially intended to be nothing more than branch lines, built to connect small towns, such as Meltham or Holmfirth, with large towns such as Huddersfield. Other branch lines originated from proposals to build shorter alternatives to existing routes, but which failed to gain acceptance. Thus the Sowerby Bridge to Rishworth branch had been part of a proposed route between Sowerby Bridge and Littleborough, which would have shortened the existing Calder valley route via Todmorden.

1914 to 2003

The network was virtually complete by the summer of 1914. The many companies, which had then existed in West Yorkshire, were grouped into two companies in 1923, and were then nationalised in 1948. Despite these changes in organisation, the railway network scarcely altered until a torrent of closures swept through West Yorkshire in the mid-1960s. Many lines were entirely closed, and of those which remained open, some intermediate stations lost their services (Figure 5.14). These closures resulted from Dr Beeching's report which stated that railways could compete with the rapidly growing use of motor vehicles, only if railways concentrated on well used long distance lines. Most of the alternative lines and branch lines built between 1849 and 1914 were axed, so the remaining network resembled that of 1849 (Figure 5.15). Following local government reorganisation in 1974, West Yorkshire Passenger Transport Authority (Metro) was established, and permitted to provide local train services. This took the form of re-opening some of the closed stations along lines which had remained open, and it brought Metro station shelters, often very different from those that had been demolished (Figures 5.13 and 5.14).

Numerous stretches of closed lines remain in the landscape as dismantled railways. Hewenden viaduct continues to enhance the landscape near Cullingworth; deep cuttings cannot be missed at Wetherby; a Pudsey embankment, reputed to be the tallest in the country, remains to cast a winter shadow. Many engineering works remain on the dismantled railway between Low Moor and Mirfield (Figure 5.16). Long stretches

Figure 5.15. *West Yorkshire Railway Network, 2001.*

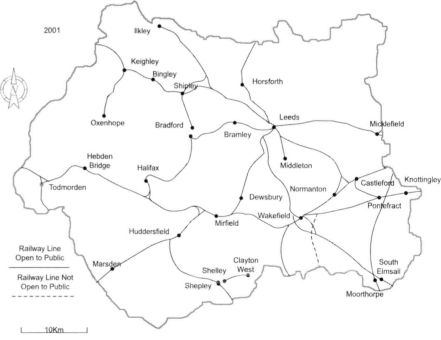

Figure 5.14. *Bramley Station 2 July 1966 when it seemed to be closing for good. A new station opened in 1983, but by then the station buildings had been demolished.*

Figure 5.16. Tunnel and cutting on the dismantled railway at Liversedge.

Figure 5.17. The Keighley and Worth Valley Railway at Oakworth.

of the dismantled railways between Low Moor and Mirfield, and between Wetherby and Spofforth, have been converted to cycleways and footpaths.

The railway lines which remain open share many landscape features, including the lines themselves, bridges, embankments, cuttings and multiple aspect signals. Some lines have steel gantries to support electric cables which provide power for electric trains (Figure 5.13). Other lines lack these features when they are worked only by diesel engines. The architecture of station buildings is the other main source of variety. Huddersfield City Council bought the splendid Huddersfield station building in 1968, and so ensured its preservation, whereas Bradford Exchange was demolished and replaced by Bradford Interchange in 1973. West Yorkshire has three preserved railways namely the Middleton, Leeds, the Kirklees Light Railway (from Shelley to Clayton West) and The Keighley and Worth Valley. The latter seeks to preserve the atmosphere of a local Edwardian railway, and some of its signals are relics of the Midland Railway (Figure 5.17). As a tourist attraction, the Keighley and Worth Valley has been helped by a direct main line connection at Keighley, and by Haworth's Bronte association. Its steam trains, and the detail of its railway landscape, not only attract visitors, but led to it being chosen as a location for the filming of *Yanks* and *The Railway Children*.

Some Sources and Further Reading

BAIRSTOW, M. *The Great Northern Railway In The West Riding*, Martin Bairstow, 1999.

CRUMP, W. B. *Huddersfield Highways Down The Ages*, The Tolson Memorial Museum, 1949.

DRAKE, M. and DRAKE, D. *Early Trackways in the South Pennines*, Pennine Heritage Network, Undated.

HADFIELD, C. *The Canals Of Yorkshire and the North East Volume I and II*, David and Charles, 1972 and 1973.

HADFIELD, C. and BIDDLE, G. *The Canals of North West England Volume I and II*, David and Charles, 1970.

HUDSON, G. *The Aberford Fly Line.* In Stevenson Tate L. *Aspects of Leeds 3*, Wharncliffe, 2001.

JOY, D. A *Regional History Of The Railways Of Great Britain Volume VIII*, South And West Yorkshire, David and Charles 1975.

RAISTRICK, A. *Green Tracks On The Pennines*, Dalesman, 1962.

SEALS, W. F. *The Leeds and Otley Turnpike*, Manuscript, 1963.

SPEAKMAN, C. *Ten Years Of Achievement*, Metro, 1985.

TAYLOR, M. The Canal and River Sections of the Aire and Calder Navigation, Wharncliffe Books, 2003.

Places to Visit

Causeways may be examined at many places including, **Farnley** (also former toll house), **Fulneck, Mankinholes** and near **Slaithwaite Hall.**

Fixby to compare an old coach road at Ochre Hole with a modern motorway.

Hipperholme to Halifax via Dark Lane. The lane was a medieval road but is now an Ancient Monument.

Otley to Lawnswood to examine the Leeds and Otley turnpike roads and their associated features.

Bingley to examine the Five Rise Locks. Can be extended to Tewitt Lane to examine a causeway.

Slaithwaite to Marsden to examine the Huddersfield Narrow Canal. The Standedge visitor centre is near Marsden. Can be extended to Close Gate Bridge (a packhorse bridge).

Walton (near Wakefield) to Cold Hiendley to examine the disused Barnsley Canal and the reservoir at Cold Hiendley.

Bradford to Huddersfield via Halifax train journey to see the problems of nineteenth century railway building in this part of the Pennines, and to compare Bradford Interchange with Huddersfield Station.

Cleckheaton to Heckmondwike to examine the landscape features of a dismantled railway.

Keighley: The Keighley and Worth Valley Railway.

THE RISE AND FALL OF TOWNS AND CITIES

WEST YORKSHIRE HAS experienced an enormous increase in its urban area and urban population size since 1379. It is equally remarkable that Pontefract and Wakefield which (with only about 1000 and 500 inhabitants) were the largest towns in 1379, are now very much smaller than Leeds and Bradford.

TOWNS BETWEEN 1066 AND 1400

Pontefract was the largest town in 1379 West Yorkshire because no other settlement possessed so important a castle, well developed craft industries and a major market. Garrisons were stationed at the castle so townspeople, including beer sellers and prostitutes, secured a living catering for the troops' needs. The castle was a frequent port of call of monarchs and nobility who increased the towns prosperity, and so encouraged the growth of craft industries, including cloth manufacture, and trade. A charter of 1257 permitted Pontefract to hold a market, and this flourished as the town was set amongst the then wealthiest and most agriculturally productive part of the county.

In contrast, Wakefield only had highly productive farmland to the east. To the west lay that part of the county which was less wealthy, and where recovery from the ravages of 1069-70 had been slow. Wakefield's castle, while it existed (it seems to have been destroyed in 1330) was less important than Pontefract's castle. However, Wakefield's administrative role and its already important craft industries made it larger than other towns except Pontefract. Wakefield not only made its own cloth, but even in 1308 possessed a cloth market, and was serving a wide area for dyeing and finishing cloth.

The manor of Wakefield and the parish of Dewsbury each extended to the Lancashire border. As transport was poorly developed, Wakefield needed centres nearer Lancashire to act as local administrative centres. Equally Dewsbury established the upper Calderdale area as a new parish. For no reason now obvious, Halifax was chosen by Wakefield to act as a local administrative centre, and by Dewsbury to have a parish church. In turn, routes developed from upper Calderdale to Halifax which promoted the settlement's commercial activities, that, by the fourteenth century, included an unlicensed market, and so initiated its urban growth.

Figure 6.1. Wetherby market place.

Halifax was unusual. During this period, other settlements became new towns through the award of a charter. Leeds was granted a borough charter in 1207. But most of the villages which became towns were awarded charters to hold a market or a fair: Almondbury in 1294, Bradford in 1251, Otley in 1227. Wetherby received its market charter in 1240, but even by 1379, the town was distinguished from surrounding villages (except Linton) merely by the presence of a few provision dealers. Nevertheless, Wetherby very slowly developed as a rural market town (Figure 6.1). Between 1400 and 1900 the degree to which towns grew (or even declined) was frequently linked to the extent to which textile industries were important in the town.

THE TEXTILE INDUSTRY FROM MEDIEVAL TIMES TO THE PRESENT DAY

The medieval importance of Pontefract for cloth making began to fade during the fifteenth century, as cloth production increased in the Pennines, despite the area's few advantages. Wool from Pennine sheep was probably used in very early times, but even as early as 1588, coarse Pennine wool went to Rochdale, whilst Calderdale received supplies of fine wool from Lincolnshire. The oft repeated claim that fast flowing streams assisted the growth of textiles is false, not least because Pennine streams are rarely naturally fast flowing. Instead, it was through people building dams and mill races that streams and rivers were able to power fulling mills. One advantage was the widespread availability of soft water, used to clean both wool and cloth; another advantage was the absence of an excessively regulated workforce. However, the key reason for increased cloth production in the Pennines was a combination of partible inheritance and population growth. Together these created ever smaller sized farms and, with a short growing season and high

rainfall, a farm size would soon be reached where a family could not be adequately fed. Before starvation set in, the family turned to making and selling increasing quantities of cloth.

Until the nineteenth century, spinning and weaving were home based. After the cloth was made it was taken to a fulling mill to be pounded in order to produce a dense finish. Certain Pennine towns were sources of wool, and centres where merchants bought cloth. Towns built piece halls and cloth halls to attract cloth trade; the first cloth hall to be built in West Yorkshire was at Heptonstall in 1558. Most piece halls and cloth halls have been wholly or partially destroyed, but Halifax retains a fine example (Figure 6.2). In some towns, merchants organised the dyeing and final finishing of the cloth.

Great changes occurred between approximately 1780 and 1850. Whilst the woollen industry remained the most important branch of the textile industry, worsted production soared, especially in Bradford, cotton manufacture developed at Todmorden and linen at Leeds. Factory production was introduced and grew ever more important. Some early factories merely brought large numbers of hand spinners and hand loom weavers together in one non-residential building. Hand loom weaving also

Figure 6.2. Halifax Piece Hall. The spire in the background is the remains of Square Church.

occurred in loom shops that were either a floor above the residential quarters of a house, or were buildings resembling small factories (Figure 6.3). Power spinning and then power loom weaving were introduced, and gradually spread, initially in worsted manufacture and later in woollens. As power processes spread, more and more factories were created to house the new, large and expensive machines. By 1850 the spinning and weaving of worsteds, and the spinning of woollens were factory based. Of the former domestic industry there remained only large numbers of handloom woollen weavers, but by 1891 even these had become uncommon. More and more textile factories, or mills as they were usually called, came to be driven by steam rather than water power.

Steam powered mills dominated the landscapes of many areas including that which lay west of central Bradford, along Bradford Beck (Figure 6.4). This zone developed because the valley floor provided gently sloping sites for easy building.

Figure 6.3. Loomshop at Addingham.

Figure 6.4. Phoenix Mill, Bradford as it was in 2002. A mill existed on this site in 1842.

The beck provided soft water which scarcely furred up the pipes in boilers. Regrettably, the beck soon became a means of disposing waste. Until 1850 all the mills were built relatively near Bradford Canal, and Bradford's railway links to Leeds and Halifax. Coal was mined in the higher parts of Bradford, and so was easily transported down slope to the valley floor. Once a few mills were built near the beck, others followed because costs could be reduced, for example, by sharing services.

West Yorkshire's textile industry continued to be important until about forty years ago when contraction became so rapid that today only a few mills still make cloth. Whilst some mills have been destroyed, others have been converted to other uses, so mills are still a feature of West Yorkshire's landscape.

URBAN GROWTH 1400 TO 1800

The urban growth of Harewood, Wetherby, Aberford and Pontefract was severely hindered by their lack, after 1400, of an expanding textile industry. The demolition of Pontefract's castle, after the Civil War, further disadvantaged the town's growth, and only the liquorice industry saved the town from utter stagnation in the eighteenth and most of the nineteenth centuries. Pontefract's economy at long last began to revive with the sinking of the first shaft of the Prince of Wales Colliery in 1870. Aberford actually ceased to be a market town about 1800, and its population size decreased in the early nineteenth century. The town's decline is rather surprising as it was located on the Great North Road where coaching traffic was on the increase in the late eighteenth century. Furthermore, coach trade had given a little fillip to Wetherby's growth at that time.

Within the area where textile production was expanding, only Wakefield and Leeds had outstanding locations for urban growth. Both towns were sited at bridging points of large rivers, and both were situated at the contact between the Pennines and the eastern lowlands. Hence, both towns were well placed to act as immediate markets for Pennine produced cloth, and best placed of all to distribute food produced in the eastern lowlands, and wool brought into West Yorkshire. Despite their similar locations, only briefly were Wakefield and Leeds of similar size. By the sixteenth century, Wakefield had become the largest town in West Yorkshire. Leeds had unexpectedly grown slowly, perhaps because the Kirkstall Abbey Cistercians had sold wool from their estates directly to markets rather than through Leeds. For whatever reasons, until the seventeenth century, the Calder valley was more developed than the Aire valley, so Wakefield was the greatest cloth centre and the largest town.

By the early seventeenth century, Leeds had caught up with, and overtaken, Wakefield to become the largest town in West Yorkshire, a position Leeds retains to this day. The dissolution of Kirkstall Abbey may have stimulated cloth production in the Aire valley, and it certainly brought land for sale in Leeds thereby attracting settlers from as far away as Carlisle and Coventry. Many of these newcomers became merchants, perhaps as a means of acquiring wealth and social standing. Newcomers directly increased the population size of Leeds, and those who were merchants created employment opportunities that brought many more people to live in Leeds. Merchants organised the dyeing and finishing of woollen cloth. These activities were relatively labour intensive, and as they grew faster at Leeds than at Wakefield, they played a key role in the more rapid growth of Leeds. Furthermore, Leeds merchants, unlike those of Wakefield, homed in on new expanding European markets for woollen cloth which brought greater industrial growth and increased population.

With the opening of the Aire and Calder Navigation (chapter five), Wakefield was the only town that might have dislodged Leeds from its premier position. And Wakefield did make some attempt by opening a cloth hall in 1710, but within a year Leeds had opened its own cloth hall. Wakefield then took a wrong turning by focusing upon the distribution of wool and of food, instead of putting even more effort into the more remunerative cloth finishing and marketing. Perhaps this change of direction was a response to the competition emanating from Halifax. Clothiers in the highly developed woollen textile industry of upper Calderdale came to Halifax to buy their wool and sell their cloth. Consequently, Halifax had grown quickly from the fifteenth century to reach a population of about 5000 in the mid-eighteenth century, and so, by then, offered stiff competition to Wakefield. In contrast, in Airedale, Bradford offered no real competition to Leeds, for Bradford had grown only slowly between the fifteenth and mid-eighteenth centuries. No convincing reason has emerged for Bradford's slow growth over those years. Wakefield's

Figure 6.5. County Hall, Wakefield.

administrative activities continued, but it was not until the nineteenth century, when it became the headquarters of the whole of the West Riding (excluding the county boroughs), that administrative work supported many people (Figure 6.5). By then it was too late to catch up, especially as Wakefield had earlier turned its back on power driven factories.

Huddersfield was granted a market in 1671, and so began to grow as a town. Prior to that year nearby Almondbury had been the region's market town, but as Huddersfield was situated at the meeting of the Colne and Holme rivers, it was far better located than upland Almondbury, particularly in the canal and railway ages (chapter five). Once Sir John Ramsden's Canal and the Huddersfield Narrow Canal were opened, Huddersfield grew rapidly both as an industrial centre itself, and as the Colne and Holme valleys' chief commercial centre. Almondbury, bypassed by the canals, then fell into relative decline.

URBAN CHANGE 1800 TO 1900
During the first decade of the nineteenth century, Huddersfield continued to grow at such a fast rate that it overtook Wakefield and Halifax to become West Yorkshire's second largest town. Huddersfield may have grown faster than Halifax because a canal opened at Huddersfield in 1776, whereas Halifax was only reached by canal in 1828. Even if this particular instance is true, the mere presence of a canal was insufficient to trigger great urban growth. A canal had reached Bradford only one year after Huddersfield, yet Bradford grew more slowly than Huddersfield, and in 1811 Bradford had not even caught up with Wakefield and Halifax.

Suddenly this was to change. Bradford's population growth rate soared between 1811 and 1831 with the result that Bradford displaced Huddersfield from second place in the urban rank order. The most likely explanation for this rapid increase in Bradford's population size is that Bradford manufacturers decided to specialise in worsted manufacture at a time when demand was rapidly increasing. Between 1822 and 1834 the number of steam powered worsted mills soared. As urban transport was scarcely developed, and what there was, expensive, mill workers had to live close to the mills, with the consequence that the number of workers' houses increased rapidly in Bradford. Immigrants were a major component of the population growth; some immigrants were from Ireland, but the great influx of Irish workers only arrived shortly after 1831.

Whilst this explanation is almost certainly true, it leaves some matters unresolved. It is doubtful if the number of mills increased sufficiently to support even half of the increased number of inhabitants. Furthermore, as most of the mill employees were women and children, it is unclear why males moved into Bradford and how they were occupied; perhaps they were labourers, hawkers and hand wool combers.

Bradford's population continued to grow, albeit at a lower rate, after 1831, as the number of textile mills and ancillary industries, such as dyeing and textile engineering, increased in the town. However, Leeds, Huddersfield and Halifax also grew, because they too attracted new industry, so the rank order, of the four largest cities, remained unchanged. In Leeds, for example, the engineering and clothing industries had grown to such an extent during the nineteenth century, that by 1901 each employed more people than the textile industry. Expanding textile industries brought growth to such smaller towns as Keighley, Bingley and Dewsbury, but their growth was never sufficient to topple the largest towns. Some manufacturers, in the third quarter of the nineteenth century, created completely new settlements such as Akroyden, Meltham Mills, Ripleyville and Saltaire, but these settlements have usually been classified as villages rather than towns, and some, such as Akroyden and Ripleyville, have become part of the urban fabric of Halifax and Bradford respectively. Numerous settlements, including Batley, Bramley, Castleford, Morley, Ossett and Pudsey, which were little more than villages when the nineteenth century opened, were converted, through the presence of growing manufacturing industries, into towns by the end of the century. Bramley failed to earn the recognition that was its due; it was the equal of Pudsey, yet it was Pudsey which was granted borough status in 1899. The rise of Ilkley, as a town, owed as much to manufacturing as Castleford, but it did so in a very different way. Once the railway reached Ilkley (in 1865) some Leeds and Bradford factory owners sought to avoid pollution, that they themselves were producing in the manufacturing towns, by living in Ilkley and travelling by train to work. The railway also enabled workers from Leeds and Bradford to take an occasional day trip to Ilkley, especially at Bank Holidays.

URBAN CHANGE 1900 TO 2000

Leeds, Bradford, Huddersfield and Halifax remain the largest towns in West Yorkshire, but within the last forty or so years (earlier in Halifax) their population sizes have declined. Many immigrants from places that included Eastern Europe, India and Pakistan settled in the towns of Yorkshire especially in the twenty or so years following 1945. In the years when immigrants were settling in cities, other citizens were either experiencing low natural increase or moving from the cities. These losses exceeded the number of immigrants, so total population declined in the large cities. People, especially businessmen and professionals, left the cities to live in what were perceived to be more pleasant environments. The population of small rural market towns such as Otley, Pontefract and Wetherby correspondingly increased, and between 1961 and 1991 the population of Wetherby more than doubled.

Virtually all West Yorkshire's towns experienced an increase in their built up areas during the twentieth century, but the increase was greatest in the largest cities (Figure 6.6). As recently as the eighteenth century, the built up area of Leeds was remarkably small. As the town's population had increased, more and more people had crammed themselves into the town centre where gardens were lost to housing. Significant outward growth only began in the nineteenth century when virtually no space was available for additional buildings in the centre. Speculative house builders were responsible for the bulk of the 1850-1925 growth of Leeds. However, in Bramley, it was the opening of two large boot factories which stimulated the erection of many nearby houses between 1881 and 1891. Despite this appreciable nineteenth century growth, it was only in the twentieth century that Leeds acquired its enormous aerial extent. Most manufacturing towns display a similar pattern of growth to that of Leeds, but in the more rural towns such as Wetherby and Pontefract, where manufacturing largely passed them by, the area of nineteenth century growth is small.

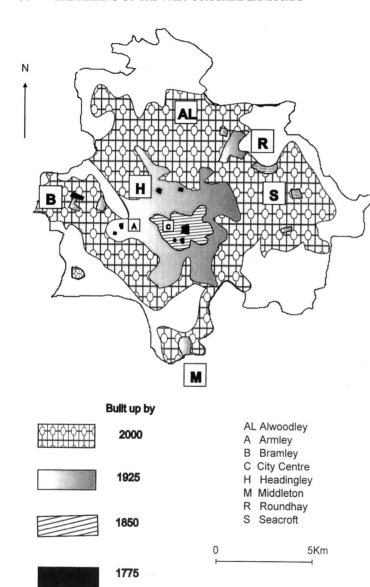

N

Built up by

	2000
	1925
	1850
	1775

AL Alwoodley
A Armley
B Bramley
C City Centre
H Headingley
M Middleton
R Roundhay
S Seacroft

0   5Km

Figure 6.6. The Growth of Leeds.

Some Sources and Further Reading

BURT, S. and GRADY, K. *The Illustrated History Of Leeds*, Breedon Books, 1994.

CRUMP, W. B. and GHORBAL, G. *History Of The Huddersfield Woollen Industry*, 1935 reprinted Kirklees Leisure Services, 1988.

FARRAR, H. *The book of Pontefract*, Barracuda Books, 1986.

FIRTH, G. *Bradford and the Industrial Revolution*, Ryburn, 1990.

FRASER, D. *A history of modern Leeds*, Manchester University Press, 1980.

GILES, C. and GOODALL, I. H. *Yorkshire Textile Mills 1770-1930*, HMSO, 1992.

HAIGH, E. A. H. *Huddersfield A Most Handsome Town*, Kirklees Cultural Services, 1992.

HARGREAVES, J. A. *Halifax*, Edinburgh University Press/Carnegie Publishing, 1999.

RICHARDSON, C. *A Geography of Bradford*, University of Bradford, 1976.

RIMMER, W. G. *The Evolution Of Leeds To 1700*, Thoresby Society Miscellany Volume 14, 1968 pp 91-129.

SILSON, A. *Bramley Takes Off* in Stevenson Tate L *Aspects of Leeds 1*, Wharncliffe, 1998.

UNWIN, R. *Wetherby The History of a Yorkshire Market Town*, Wetherby Historical Trust, 1986.

WATERS, S. H. *Wakefield In The Seventeenth Century*, Sanderson and Clayton, 1933.

Places to Visit

Bradford to visit the Moorside Industrial Museum; the mills outwards from the city centre along Thornton Road; Lister's Manningham Mill and nearby terraced houses.

Halifax to observe the Piece Hall; Dean Clough Mills; Akroyden (a model village).

Ilkley to examine a nineteenth century commuter town and small resort.

Either Otley or Wetherby to visit the market place and the bridge over the Wharfe. (In each town the bridge is an Ancient Monument).

Saltaire to explore this model village built by Sir Titus Salt, and which, in 2002, acquired World Heritage status.

Wakefield particularly to observe the administrative quarter of the Town Hall, County Hall and the West Riding Register of Deeds Office.

URBAN LANDSCAPES

THE CITY OF Leeds comprises a central area characterised by a concentration of tall buildings primarily occupied by shops and offices, but with a number of recently built flats; an inner city of mixed residential buildings and terraced houses; a suburban region of semi-detached and detached houses. Within these broad areas, there are detailed variations such as the presence of some terraced houses in the suburbs. Factories and warehouses occupy certain parts of the city beyond the central area (chapter eight). All these landscapes exist in other West Yorkshire towns and cities, though some are poorly represented in certain towns. Accordingly Leeds, as delimited by its 1973 County Borough boundary (Figure 6.6), has been selected to exemplify West Yorkshire's urban landscapes and other towns will be mentioned only when their landscapes differ markedly from those of Leeds.

THE CENTRAL AREA FROM 1822 TO 1939

In 1822 a commercial core extended approximately from Park Row to Vicar Lane and from the Upper and Lower Headrows to Boar Lane (Figure 7.1). Turnpike roads focused upon this core, making it the most accessible part of Leeds and, in turn, the main shopping area. However, financial and legal offices, workshops and houses jostled with shops for space. During the nineteenth century, horse bus routes and tram routes developed, but as they also focused upon the central area, it remained the most accessible part of Leeds. Consequently, as trade increased, competition for sites within the central area grew, and land values rose. In order to maximise the use of such high value land, tall buildings were erected.

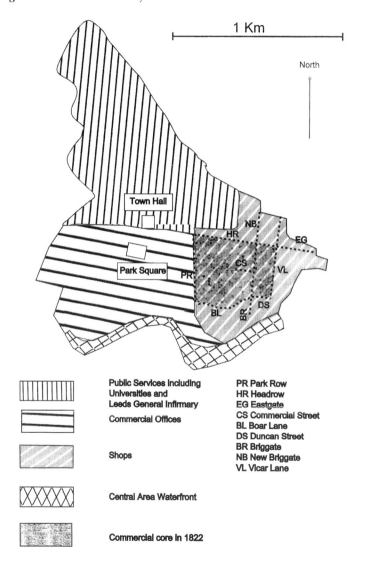

Figure 7.1. *The central area of Leeds in 1822 and 2002.*

Public Services including Universities and Leeds General Infirmary	PR Park Row
	HR Headrow
Commercial Offices	EG Eastgate
	CS Commercial Street
Shops	BL Boar Lane
	DS Duncan Street
	BR Briggate
Central Area Waterfront	NB New Briggate
	VL Vicar Lane
Commercial core in 1822	

Large parts of the commercial core were redeveloped between 1875 and 1909. Charles Thornton was a pioneer who converted the Talbot Yard into a shopping arcade in 1878. Later, other arcades were built, and much old property was replaced by new. Many houses, workshops, commercial offices and banks were replaced by shops, though the Bank of England had relocated to Park Row as early as 1864. The demand for extra shops had arisen from an increase in wealth and population size. Shops sought sites of the highest accessibility because such sites maximised their number of customers. As the commercial core was the most accessible part of Leeds, shops outbid other users for sites in the core, which thus came to be predominantly occupied by shops.

Commercial offices and banks followed the lead of the Bank of England, and by the early twentieth century were to be found on, or close to, Park Row. This locality was near to large numbers of shops which provided the banks with considerable business. Large buildings, designed to impress customers, were erected by banks and insurance companies along Park Row. If anything, taller buildings were erected in the office area rather than in the shopping area. Any such early twentieth century contrast appears to have heightened in recent years.

Leeds Corporation also played a role in developing the landscapes of the central area. The height and the splendour of the Town Hall, erected in 1858, reflected civic pride in the importance of Leeds, as, in a different style, did the Civic Hall opened in 1933. The Corporation had, at various times, widened roads, but its greatest achievement came in the 1930s when the Upper and Lower Headrows were widened to form today's Headrow. Buildings were demolished on the northern side of the two Headrows and the Corporation insisted that replacement buildings, by the widened Headrow, had to have a common elevation and frontage. By this insistence some of Leeds' most handsome buildings were erected.

THE CENTRAL AREA TODAY

Most of today's street plan not only resembles that visible in 1939, but the narrow streets, yards and arcades found within the shopping district actually have a medieval origin. When a 'new' town of Leeds was laid out in 1207, plots of land were arranged approximately at right angles to Briggate, which was planned to be the main street. During the nineteenth century, one of these burgage plots was altered to create Commercial Street. The plots were reached by paths which later became yards, some of which, such as Turk's Head Yard, still remain, but others were converted into arcades in the nineteenth century.

Since 1939, terraced houses and derelict land in the northern part of the central area have been replaced by the two universities and the Merrion Shopping Centre. The building occupied by Leeds Metropolitan University was built tall to enable large numbers of students to be taught on high value land. Elsewhere in the central area, shop frontages have changed, and some banks and offices have become bars and restaurants. Many buildings have been renovated, a recent example is that now known as The Light. Numerous buildings have been demolished and replaced by new ones, for example, Schofield's department store has been replaced by The Headrow Centre.

Despite losses, large numbers of pre-1939 buildings still remain, a testament to their high quality, and the small degree of war-time bomb damage. Furthermore, in what seemed to be a widespread sixties phase by local authorities to clear older properties, Leeds just managed to retain its market buildings, but Bradford Council had its Kirkgate Market building demolished. In Halifax just one vote saved the Piece Hall from an identical fate. An Act of 1967 allowed local authorities to designate certain localities as Conservation Areas in which the landscape would be either preserved or enhanced. Albion Place, with its numerous Victorian and Edwardian buildings, is but one of many Conservation Areas within Leeds.

Land values remain high in the central area. Consequently, newly erected buildings are at least as tall, if not taller, than their predecessors (Figure 7.2). Shops and offices continue to predominate because many people still use public transport either to shop or to reach their workplace, and bus routes continue to make the central area the most accessible part of the city. In the near future, this high level of accessibility looks as though it will be maintained by the opening of a Supertram. This whole process is self-reinforcing because it is the very presence of so many shops and offices that leads bus routes to focus upon this part of the city. Leeds Council has played a role

Figure 7.2. City Square, Leeds. Photographed in 2003, after its recent renovation.

in maintaining the status quo, as it has not particularly encouraged out of town shopping developments. Moreover, in 1951, council planners took the then existing central area landscapes and, with a little tidying, decided that those existing spatial patterns should continue into the future.

However, the Council has permitted substantial changes in the waterfront landscapes. The area was Leeds' dockland, initially created by the Aire and Calder Navigation, but by about 1960 it had become derelict, unattractive and unwanted. Leeds Development Corporation, which worked with the Council and private bodies, transformed the area. Asda relocated its head offices from Kirkstall Road to the waterfront, and so set the ball rolling. A few cranes, wharves and stone warehouses can still be seen, but most of the industrial premises have been converted or rebuilt to create attractive riverside flats. These have been particularly developed for young executives working in the nearby expanding commercial office area. Redevelopment is currently underway in the West End between Wellington Street, Wellington Bridge and the waterfront. In 2002, on the former Whitehall electricity power station site, a tall building, designed to be an hotel, offices and flats, was completed. New offices are being built to provide better facilities than those in older offices located away from the waterfront.

Many of these central area changes preceded, but have been in accord with, a mid-1990s central government recommendation that local authorities should encourage new central area development. It is believed that central area services should be at least maintained and capable of competing with out of town developments. People should also be able to live in central areas to enable them to travel on foot to work and to urban recreational facilities, and thereby reduce motor vehicle usage. Within this climate, and given the success of the waterfront development, new flats, such as K2 Albion Street, and, on the margin of the central area, Aspect 14 Lovell Park Road, have been recently erected.

No other West Yorkshire town has a waterfront quite like that of Leeds, partly because no other town combines a former large dockland with a nearby expanding office industry which employs many affluent workers. Of West Yorkshire's urban central areas, only Leeds has so many really tall buildings, because only in Leeds has the service sector grown to such an extent that there is immense competition for space and such correspondingly high land values. Indeed, some of the smallest towns, such as Castleford and Wetherby, scarcely have an office quarter at all, and their shopping districts are small with buildings of low elevation. However, the central area of Leeds lacks the tall stone built warehouses that so dominate parts of the central areas of the former great woollen and worsted towns of Dewsbury and Bradford.

INNER CITY LANDSCAPES

The inner city is here delimited as that part of Leeds, outside the central area, that was chiefly built between 1775 and 1925 (Figure 6.6 and 7.1). The pre-1850 area consisted of narrow streets or yards which were occupied by back to back houses. Quite often each house was no more than an up and a down, but it might have to sleep up to twelve people. Ventilation, drainage and clean water supplies were conspicuous by their absence, and under such conditions cholera and other diseases readily took their toll. Even by 1860 such neighbourhoods were being identified as slums, but clearance was pitifully slow and many districts were not demolished until the 1960s.

In their place, the Council has erected a great variety of house types. Scattered multi-storey blocks of flats tower above short terraces, a few bungalows and semi-detached houses in such

Figure 7.3. A redevelopment landscape at Burmantofts.

localities as Burmantofts and New Wortley (Figure 7.3). The flats were built to create an overall lower density of buildings than formerly existed, yet to enable large numbers of people to be accommodated. They were also built because flats were very fashionable amongst 1960s councils. Whilst a number of tall blocks of flats have been recently erected by private builders on, and near, the waterfront and where the central area gives way to the inner city, multi-story council flats have proved to be unpopular and already have been demolished at Beeston and Swarcliffe. The new flats are close to office work and city night life, whereas the older flats can be in the heart of the inner city. Security and household facilities are likely to be better in the new flats than in the old. These contrasts might go some way towards accounting for the differences in popularity of the two sets of high rise flats. Nevertheless, new multi-story flats also occur at Headingley, so not all such flats are within a short walking distance of the city centre.

Unlike the older terraced houses, large areas of terraced houses built after 1880 still exist as they were of better quality than the older properties. Bye-laws, introduced in 1870, led to two up and two down back to backs with, usually after every fourth house, a yard initially for privies and later for shared WCs (Figure 7.4). A few back to backs were built with indoor WCs. Access to the rear of many Bradford and Huddersfield back to backs was gained by a passage built after every two houses, but such a style was rare in Leeds.

Figure 7.4. Back to backs in Burley.

Many through terraces, which were better ventilated than back to backs, were also built. Since 1960 both types of terraced house have been in steady demand to house newly arrived immigrants, first time home buyers and, in recent years, students.

Terraced houses continued to be built after 1870 because land costs per house were low, especially as they were built either without gardens or with only minute gardens. Building costs per house were also low, particularly in back to backs where walls were shared between up to three houses. As houses were relatively inexpensive, landlords could still make a handsome profit from the low rents which were all poorly paid workers could afford. Only small numbers of industrial workers lived in Wetherby so relatively few terraced houses were built in the town.

A rectilinear street pattern was laid out, partly because it is easier to build terraces along straight streets than curved ones, but largely because Leeds Corporation bye-laws insisted that roads had to intersect at right angles and an intersection had to occur every one hundred and fifty yards. Some streets followed medieval open field strips in parts of Little London (Leeds) prior to redevelopment and in certain streets in Manningham, Bradford.

THE SUBURBS

Contemporary suburban areas are characterised by the presence of large numbers of semi-detached and detached houses set amongst small to moderate sized gardens (Figure 7.5). A suburb had developed in the nineteenth century at Headingley by the well to do moving up from the western end of Leeds to avoid its billowing smoke. Late in the nineteenth century, Chapel Allerton was changing into a suburb as the more upwardly mobile members of the working

Figure 7.5. *Inter-war semi-detached houses at Gledhow.*

class sought to inhabit better houses. However, most of today's great swathe of suburban housing has been built since 1925 (Figure 6.6). House building spread beyond the inner city in the inter-war period when there were few planning restrictions, farming was depressed and agricultural land was, accordingly, cheaply available for building. In 1947 central government dealt planners a stronger hand, but, until 1970, Leeds Council was usually more ready to allow building than to conserve the countryside. Indeed the Council itself was a major builder of houses between 1920 and 1970 as it sought to provide improved housing for the overcrowded and the slum dwellers. Cleared areas could not re-house everyone in low density housing, so new estates had to be built on greenfield sites. Private builders also sought to provide improved housing, but their targeted groups were the upwardly mobile working class and the middle class. Building Societies were usually ready to make loans to builders of such houses, and to offer mortgages to home owners. The need for new houses was also a result of a fall in average household size.

It was only possible for such vast areas of low density housing to exist because land values were far lower in this urban outer zone than elsewhere in the city and because twentieth century transport changes enabled people to live at considerable distances from their workplaces.

The vast increase in the area occupied by housing is more readily explained than the particular house styles which were created. The building of back to backs had been banned from 1909, though a loophole enabled a few to be built until 1937. However, large quantities of high quality terraced houses, along with medium sized gardens could have been built, but instead, builders mostly opted for semi-detached houses up to about 1975. Inter-war advertising helped to promote the desirability of living in a detached or at least a semi-detached house. The large numbers of semis then erected were visible compromises between the desirable detached house and money available to buy or rent a house.

Council built semi-detached houses display subtle differences from privately built semis. Council semi-detached houses were usually built without bay windows; some were almost entirely made of concrete, which was rarely the case in privately built houses. Private builders of nineteenth century terraced houses often opted to build in brick in Leeds, but in stone in Bradford and Huddersfield, and a similar contrast is visible in a number of privately built twentieth century semi-detached houses. Many council estates were varied by the sporadic occurrence of multi-story flats, but these were absent from private estates. Straight streets are to be found on some private estates, but curvaceous streets can occur on either private or council estates. Some of the latter are further distinguished by the presence of radial streets that cut across streets shaped as concentric circles. Fashions change, and since the mid-seventies, private builders, but not the Council, have erected a number of detached houses particularly in the outer parts of the city. (Figure 7.6).

Since 1974, planners have successfully prevented much building from occurring on the greatly enlarged greenbelt area that became part of Leeds, following local government re-organisation. Consequently, there has been a shortage of extensive greenfield building sites. This has led builders to search for every possible plot, however small, they can find, and much recent building has been the infilling of gaps in an already existing housing area. In this way, some fields and open spaces have continued to be lost to builders. Infill has contributed to the presence of local variations within the inner city and the suburbs. Another reason for such variations is the presence of long established settlements within the former borough of Leeds. Bramley is one such old town. It has diversified the broad suburban region of Leeds by its small 1970s redeveloped shopping and residential core, and a pre-1920s zone of terraced houses.

Figure 7.6. Detached houses at Adel.

Some Sources and Further Reading

BAINES, EDWARD. *History and Directory of the County of York*, Edward Baines, 1822.

BERESFORD, M. W. and JONES, G. R. J. *Leeds And Its Region*, (details in chapter two).

CAFFYN, L. *Workers' Housing in West Yorkshire, 1750-1920*, HMSO, 1986.

GODWARD, B. *Leeds Heritage Trail*, Leeds Civic Trust, 2000.

PLOWS, M. *Roundhay Hall: A Personal History* in Stevenson Tate L *Aspects of Leeds 3*, Wharncliffe, 2001.

SILSON, A. *Bramley Half A Century Of Change*, Anthony Silson, 1993.

VARO, S. *A Mercantile Meander*, Stanley Varo, 1989.

(Books by Burt S, and Grady K, Fraser D and Richardson C listed in chapter six are also relevant here).

Places to Visit

Bradford to examine warehouses in Little Germany and to walk from Wapping to Fagley to examine different types of terraced houses.

Dewsbury to examine warehouses in the central area.

Huddersfield for a short walk from Wakefield Road, along Mayfield Avenue and Dalton Green Lane, which reveals a large variety of different house types.

Leeds

1. A waterfront walk from Granary Wharf to the Royal Armouries.
2. Explore the area bounded by City Square, Millennium Square, The Grand Theatre and Kirkgate Market to experience landscape contrasts in the central area of Leeds.
3. Burmantofts for inner city redevelopment.
4. Burley for nineteenth century terraced houses.
5. Holt Park and Adel for council and private suburban housing.
6. Bramley for 1970s council shopping centre redevelopment.

MODERN INDUSTRY IN THE LANDSCAPE

MODERN INDUSTRY IS enormously diverse. Quarrying is now rare, but some quarries, including those at Hawksworth and Morley, are open. Agriculture and outdoor recreational industries will be discussed in chapters nine and ten, whilst retailing and office activities were partly discussed in chapter seven. Consequently, this chapter focuses upon manufacturing, but it also includes recent developments in warehouses, offices and shops located outside the central areas of towns and cities. Even within these parameters, a selective approach has had to be taken.

Many contemporary industrial premises were not only built years ago, but they owe their presence to factors that are no longer relevant. The oldest of the industries to be discussed is flour milling. Some corn mills such as Watson's, near Sowerby Bridge, became textile mills, but most of these developed in their own right after 1800. The presence of a textile industry then promoted the growth of a chemical industry. Later still, industrial and domestic demand led to the construction of thermal power stations. These four industries have been chosen to illustrate how manufacturing came to be located in West Yorkshire, why it continues, and how certain manufacturing processes have produced particular landscape features.

Within the last thirty or so years, very different industrial landscapes have developed. New industrial premises display a much greater similarity in appearance than older premises, and new types of industrial location have come into existence. These significant landscape changes constitute the later part of this chapter.

FLOUR MILLS

Queen's Mill, Castleford, and King's Mill, Knottingley, are splendid, but very different, survivors of West Yorkshire's once widespread corn milling industry (Figure 8.1). Mills have been in existence at these sites since medieval times. Both mills were rebuilt in the late nineteenth century, and since then, Queen's Mill has not been altered, whereas King's Mill has, in recent years, acquired huge towers. Each mill once had a range of locational advantages, but by 1970 scarcely any of these remained. Whereas in the eighteenth century, locally grown grain was milled, today large quantities of grain are imported, especially to Queen's Mill which, for its bread flour, must use hard wheat, for example, from Canada. Loading bays (Figure 8.1a) show Queen's Mill once used the Aire and Calder Navigation for transport, as did King's Mill, but today, both use road transport. Originally the mills were driven by water wheels, and amazingly water power was used at Queen's Mill until 1970; since then, the mill has been powered by electricity. However, proposals exist for the water wheel to again work Queen's Mill, and for the waterway to once more transport goods to and from the mills. The flour that, in medieval times, supplied local markets is now sold locally and nationally. Queen's Mill even exports flour to the Middle East.

Both mills are now owned by one firm, Allied Mills, but are each able to continue because their methods and products are complementary. Queen's Mill has survived because its traditionally produced stone ground wholemeal flour is in great demand as a health food. Although King's Mill does not make such specialised flour, the mill is viable because milling is completely computerised and so production costs are very low.

(a)

(b)

Figure 8.1. *(a) Queen's Mill. (b) King's Mill. Note both mills are tall to enable grain to be stored and to be processed preparatory to milling. Although the industry is old, the right hand tower at King's Mill has been very recently built.*

TEXTILE MILLS

Between 1790 and 1920, huge numbers of textile mills were erected in an area south of a line from Keighley to Leeds and west of a line from Leeds to Denby Dale. This area possessed advantages that permitted this great expansion of the industry, and enabled the mills to be widely scattered. The presence of many streams and rivers allowed large numbers of water powered mills, including Bridgehouse, Haworth, to be built. As ever more steam powered mills opened, the area's proximity to coal, and its large quantities of soft water, which slowed the rate at which the pipes in a boiler furred up, proved to be great assets. Some steam powered mills including Hopton, Mirfield, and Calder Bank, Dewsbury, were built in valley floors, but steam power and later electrical power, enabled many mills, including Black Dyke, Queensbury, and Empire, Bramley, to be built well away from rivers.

Empire Mills, which opened in 1915, is one of a handful of mills that continue solely to make textiles. As to the other mills, some have been demolished, and many have survived by accommodating different industries. Armley Mills and Thwaite Mills are industrial museums; Robin Mills, at Greengates, is occupied by printers who relocated from Rawdon to obtain more space, and Castleton Mills, Leeds is occupied by a data communications systems business. Many mills have been divided into separate industrial units, and at Black Dyke Mills, workshop, warehouse and office units have been made in the belief that diversity will bring commercial success. Yet others have survived by their conversion to flats. Good examples include the former Firth Street Mills, located by a canal in the centre of Huddersfield and the former Ellar Carr Mills, Cullingworth.

Textile mills are often made of stone, sometimes of brick, but they are characterised by their large number of windows; a few retain a large window which aided perchers in their search for, and correction of, minute flaws in cloth. Different phases of growth and different processes have led to great diversity within and amongst mill landscapes. Common components, not all of which are necessarily present in any given mill, are a multi-storeyed mill used for fulling, scribbling and spinning, a weaving shed, a warehouse and offices. Calder Bank Mills reveals a clear contrast between a tall warehouse, and one storey sheds with their distinctive saw-toothed roofs. Such roofs provided top lighting, which made it easier than side lighting to detect any faults in the cloth as it was being woven. A one storeyed shed could accommodate large numbers of power looms, and yet minimise the risk of structural damage from the vibration established when the looms operated.

CHEMICAL MANUFACTURING

Most chemical works are a mass of different sized buildings, connecting pipes, storage tanks and up-right cylinders (Figure 8.2). The presence, on a given site, of so many different units reflects the varied chemical processes that occur within the works, and the wide range of ancillary activities, such as laboratories and offices, that support manufacturing. Should a fire break out, it might be more easily contained when buildings are separate. Many works have an approximately rectilinear plan which was established to aid the movement of commodities about the works. Part of the Dalton works has a remarkably rectilinear plan which, when it was designed in 1915, was deliberately copied from that of a large works at Leverkusen. It was hoped that such a plan would help the works to achieve maximum output in order to contribute to Britain's war effort.

Figure 8.2. *Part of the huge chemical works at Dalton, Huddersfield.*

The demand for chemicals grew in the nineteenth century as other industries, particularly textiles, expanded. A dyestuffs works opened in Leeds in 1820. Ammonia (used for scouring in the woollen industry) was made in Huddersfield from 1830 and in Wakefield from 1840. Later both towns made artificial dyestuffs. Ammonia and artificial dyes were derived from coal, so the many coal mines in West Yorkshire were of enormous benefit to the industry. Coal was also used as a source of power. The First World War increased the demand for chemicals, and led to the building of new chemical works at Dalton, Deighton and Castleford. In the inter-war period, the dyestuffs industry was saved by government imposed restriction on imports. Since 1945, West Yorkshire's chemical industry has survived by securing world-wide markets and by varying its product range.

Many major chemical works are located in large valley floors, but the works at Castleford Ings has more site advantages than any of the other works. Ernest Hickson already had a chemical works at Wakefield, in late 1914, when the government allowed the firm to make explosives, but the site was too small and could not be reached by rail. So a new chemical works was erected in 1915 at Castleford Ings, where a railway siding already reached an existing works, and where the River Aire supplied water and enabled waste to be carried away. The Aire and Calder Navigation was available for transport, and during the 1920s was used to bring nitric acid, imported from Norway, to the works. Chemical works are not always found in valleys; the large chemical works at Wyke, Bradford, has an elevated site that is nowhere near a river or canal, and is without direct access to a railway.

THERMAL POWER PRODUCTION AT FERRYBRIDGE

Electricity production commenced at Ferrybridge in 1927. It was then one of many small West Yorkshire power stations which were mainly located near their respective urban markets. The electricity industry was nationalised in 1948, and this brought a much improved national grid to transport electricity in the 1950s. Small high cost urban power stations were then gradually closed as production came to be concentrated upon a few large low cost producers. Ferrybridge was the only West Yorkshire power station to be selected for massive expansion, principally because there was plenty of unused land on the site and it was located in the area where coal mining was becoming concentrated. The present vast works at Ferrybridge were under construction between 1962 and 1967 (Figure 8.3).

In 2001 Ferrybridge Power Station was near, and connected by rail, to West Yorkshire's only remaining deep mined coal at Pontefract and to North Yorkshire's deep mined Selby coal. At St. Aidan's open cast working, coal was very cheaply obtained because, once the overburden had been stripped off, the coal was loose enough to be dug out (Figure 8.4). From St Aidan's,

Figure 8.3. Ferrybridge Power Station.

Figure 8.4. St Aidan's great open cast working in September 2001. Production ended in December 2002 and by May 2003 large parts were already infilled.

the coal was cheaply transported by the environmentally friendly Aire and Calder Navigation to Ferrybridge. Regrettably, Ferrybridge may soon be entirely dependent upon imported coal because both St Aidan's and the Prince of Wales colliery, Pontefract, ceased producing coal in 2002 and the Selby coalfield could cease production soon. An open cast working at Moss Carr, near Methley, that is currently supplying coal to Ferrybridge, is expected to end during 2004.

As Ferrybridge was designed to consume large amounts of coal, two very tall chimneys were erected to disperse smoke and gases (Figure 8.3). The turbines are steam driven, so large quantities of water are consumed. This water is extracted from the Aire and Calder Navigation, and to enable it to be returned to the Navigation, eight enormous towers were built to cool steam (Figure 8.3). Construction of the cooling towers was aided by the flat flood plain site.

OVENDEN MOOR WIND FARM

Thermal power stations increase the amount of carbon dioxide in the atmosphere and thereby probably contribute to global warming. They also increase rainfall acidity. Recently, people have sought more environmentally friendly methods of generating electricity, and as a contribution towards meeting this aim, a wind farm began to generate electricity on Ovenden Moor in 1993 (Figure 8.5).

Figure 8.5. Ovenden Moor Wind Farm.

Sails are attached to each of the tall towers. When the wind blows, and reaches a minimum speed of five metres per second, the sails turn, and so generate electricity in a box attached to the tower. Ovenden Moor was chosen as a site for a wind farm because of its high altitude. In inland areas, the requisite wind speed is more likely to be reached on more occasions at high altitudes than at low ones. In addition, the prevailing south westerly winds have a comparatively even flow here because there are no higher areas immediately to the south west.

RECENTLY ERECTED MANUFACTURING AND WAREHOUSE PREMISES

Factories and warehouses erected within the last dozen or so years are characterised by their uniform appearance. Each building has a gently pitched roof, a low elevation, few, if any, windows, and is no more than a steel girder shell cladded by corrugated steel, perhaps with a brick or stone base and with a concrete floor (Figure 8.6). Cladding can be bought in various sizes, and so can be readily added to different sized steel units. Construction is simple and rapid, and consequently, labour costs are minimised. Costs are further reduced, and security enhanced, by the paucity of windows; light is obtained either when large entrance shutters are raised or by electric roof lights. Warehouses and factories are virtually identical, but sometimes factories can be distinguished by the presence of chimneys. Some of these recently built premises either form complete factories in themselves or are extensions to existing works. Differently designed new premises do occasionally arise to meet the demands of particular manufacturing processes or particular industrial functions. Brewing has been selected to illustrate the role of manufacturing processes, and ice cream to illustrate the role of functions.

Figure 8.6. A modern industrial unit at Morley.

BREWING

Many minute breweries have recently been established in West Yorkshire. They either occupy older industrial buildings, including a former dyehouse in Dewsbury, or they are a part of public house premises, such as the former stables occupied by The Boat Brewery, Allerton Bywater (Figure 8.7a). Consequently, these breweries usually maintain, rather than change, the landscape.

At the other extreme is the enormous Carlsberg-Tetley Brewery near Crown Point Bridge, Leeds, where a brewery has existed for over two centuries. Taylor's Knowle Spring Brewery, Keighley, is medium sized and has existed on that site since 1863. Both breweries were established at their respective sites in order to use their reliable supplies of high quality underground water. Knowle Spring Brewery retains many of its nineteenth century buildings, but includes some recent, tall, corrugated steel ones designed to aid brewing (Figure 8.7b). Carlsberg-Tetley's brewery has been virtually rebuilt, but some components, such as its tall cylindrical tanks, have a form far removed from recently built general purpose industrial premises. The brewery serves national markets, so a large distribution centre has been recently built on a former colliery site at Tingley by junction 28 of the M62.

ICE CREAM

During the 1990s, a farm at Shelley, one at Tong and another at Whitley each established a cafe selling home made ice cream. Today, Shelley and Whitley cafes continue to sell ice cream made from milk from the farms' own dairy herds. The Tong cafe is housed in a converted farm building that is now low and made of stone, whilst that at Shelley occupies a modern corrugated steel clad unit which harmonises with the other farm buildings. Different yet again is the Whitley Cafe and its grounds which include a children's play area and pet animals.

Figure 8.7. (a) The Boat, a new brewery in an old building. (b) Knowle Spring, an old brewery with new units.

Figure 8.8. Ice Cream Cafe, Whitley.

These premises were designed with the prime aim of attracting customers and so, of the three cafes, it is Whitley that is most conspicuous. And it is only at Whitley that the selling of ice cream has markedly influenced building type (Figure 8.8). Whilst the Shelley business developed to use surplus milk, the Whitley concern arose when one partner, who had run a haulage business, sought a complete change and decided to keep cows. The availability of Jersey milk led to the making, and then the road side selling, of ice cream. This business prospered and so an ice cream cafe was constructed and then opened.

RECENTLY BUILT OFFICES AND SHOPS

Many offices, built in the early nineties, resemble overgrown houses with their brick walls, numerous windows and slate roofs. Offices built even more recently, show similarities to new factories and warehouses with their gently pitched roofs, partly cladded steel girder shell and low elevations. They differ from factories and warehouses by usually possessing numerous windows, and sometimes by their curvaceous roofs and a cladding of pale terracotta tiles (Figure 8.9).

Such offices are at least as visually attractive as many recently built shopping centres, some of which, apart from the presence of large windows, might well be warehouses or factories. Crown Point Retail Park, Leeds, is a case in point, whilst one of the shops at Owlcotes Centre, Pudsey, has windows only in the roof. Car parks have become prominent features of the landscapes of new offices and shopping centres, as their presence encourages business people to occupy the premises and attracts customers. Attempts have also been made to attract customers to shops, and to create a more pleasant working environment for office workers, by planting trees near shop and office premises (Figure 8.9).

NEW LOCATIONS FOR INDUSTRIAL PREMISES

Motorways have played a major role in locating industry ever since the first West Yorkshire motorway opened in 1971. Within the last twenty or so years, large numbers of industrial premises have been built close to motorways on greenfield sites near Oakenshaw, Morley, Outwood, Normanton and Stourton. All these localities have gently sloping sites which people were prepared to sell or lease, and which were granted

Figure 8.9. An office at Paragon Business Park, near Outwood.

Mail relocated from the centre of Leeds to Stourton because its Leeds premises had insufficient ground floor space for its new large machines, whilst these could be readily accommodated in new premises at Stourton.

Certain inner city sites, which are near motorways, have also experienced recent land use changes, for example, Crown Point Retail Park occupies former railway sidings. Within the last decade, offices have begun to invade inner city Hunslet partly to mitigate parking problems in Leeds city centre, but chiefly because the centre had insufficient high quality office space.

Despite the key role played by motorways in recent industrial location, some new industrial premises, particularly those for indoor recreation and shopping, have been located away from motorways. Leeds Road, Huddersfield, and Thornbury, Bradford, both have cinemas; some land near the Stanningley bypass is occupied by the Owlcotes shopping centre, and Kirkstall valley has both a cinema and shopping centre. These activities are located on lower land value sites away from city centres, but close to large numbers of residents who can reach these service centres by main roads. Motorways are not essential because such businesses are primarily seeking to serve customers within a short drive of their premises.

planning permission for industrial use. Wakefield Council has actively encouraged new industrial growth to try to compensate for the economic loss sustained by coal mine closures. Sites near Leeds have been sought because Leeds is the economic heart of West Yorkshire. The margins of Leeds have proved attractive to space consuming activities, as land values are lower in the margins than in the centre. The Royal

Some Sources and Further Reading

There does not appear to be any one published book that discusses all the topics examined in this chapter. Even books on individual industries are rare. Though not used as sources, ALASTAIR LAURENCE'S *History Of Pool Paper Mills*, 1986 and JOHN CHARTRES and KATRINA HONEYMAN'S *Leeds City Business,* 1993 may prove useful further reading.

HOLME, I. *A Centenary History of the Dyeing and Finishing Industry Huddersfield Region,* Society of Dyers and Colourists, 1988 has been a useful, but highly specialised source.

WALKER, R. *Born and Brewed in Yorkshire,* Wharncliffe, 2001 briefly describes Yorkshire's independent breweries.

Apart from these books and some others listed in chapter six, most of the material for this chapter has been obtained from

i) fieldwork, including asking business people questions;
ii) various maps;
iii) various articles and newspaper reports;
iv) handbooks such as HODSMAN H.J. *Society of Chemical Industry Handbook for the 44th Annual Meeting,* Leeds, 1925;
v) directories; business guides and market research reports;
vi) a biography of Ernest Hickson written by his son, (manuscript c.1967).

Places to Visit

Armley Mills Industrial Museum or **Thwaite Mills Industrial Museum.**

Castleford and **Knottingley** to compare the site and appearance of Queen's Mill and King's Mill.

Dalton Nature Reserve, Huddersfield, provides a superb bird's eye view of Dalton Chemical works.

Dewsbury to observe Calder Bank Mills.

Ferrybridge to examine the site of the power station.

One of: **Morley, Outwood, Normanton** to look at the type of buildings found in an industrial estate, and to examine its site.

Ovenden Moor Wind Farm where there is a display and viewing platform.

Treat yourself to an ice cream at **Shelley, Tong and Whitley.**

THE MODERN RURAL LANDSCAPE

SUMMER IS THE best season to observe the county's major contrasts in rural land use. At that time, purple heather gives way to green grass in the west, whilst yellows dominate as cereals ripen in the east. These very different landscapes are mainly a response to contemporary circumstance. However, existing field patterns and rural settlements demand an historical perspective to assist in their interpretation. This chapter illustrates how both past and present processes have created the modern rural landscape.

VILLAGES

The rural settlement pattern of single houses, hamlets and villages was firmly established by the mid-nineteenth century and has scarcely altered since then (chapter four). Many scattered rural houses remain, even though their occupants no longer work the land, because motor cars enable numbers of retired people or commuters to enjoy a relatively isolated existence. Villages also continue to exist, but their forms have considerably changed during the twentieth century. Three broad groups of village form may be recognised. In a linear form, buildings are arranged in a row, whereas in a compact form, buildings cluster together (Figure 9.1). A linear form becomes branched when several roads meet at a village and when buildings are strung along more than one road. These three types can each be subdivided into villages which possess a green and those which do not (Figure 9.2).

In 1775 the majority of West Yorkshire's villages were either linear or branched. Compact forms are now more significant because linear and branched villages have either grown into compact villages or been absorbed within cities as these have expanded. One of the few villages to have retained its linear form is Tong (Figure 9.1a). Sir George Tempest owned Tong Hall, the park in which it was located, and a large area surrounding the park in the early eighteenth century. It was during this period of prosperity that Sir George effectively built the village of Tong. Houses were built along part of Tong Lane which itself follows the crest of a spur. The linear form then founded, remained scarcely altered until the late twentieth century. Colonel Plumb Tempest, a nineteenth century owner of Tong Estate, was recorded as being totally opposed to the village of Tong acquiring new buildings and becoming yet another manufacturing village. Assuming the Tempests who succeeded Colonel Plumb Tempest held similar views, the stability of Tong until 1935 is largely accounted for. A local

Figure 9.1. (a) Tong: a linear village; (b) East Keswick: a compact village.

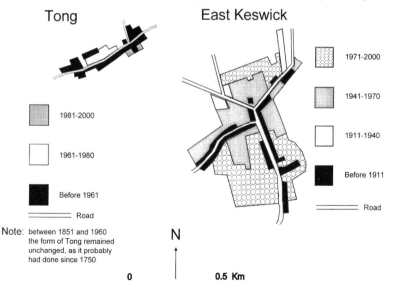

Tong

East Keswick

	1971-2000
	1941-1970
	1911-1940
	Before 1911
═══	Road

1981-2000

1961-1980

Before 1961

═══ Road

Note: between 1851 and 1960 the form of Tong remained unchanged, as it probably had done since 1750

N

0   0.5 Km

businessman bought part of the estate in 1935 and the remainder in 1941. By then, the Second World War precluded the building of large numbers of new houses, and so kept Tong unchanged for a number of years.

Since the strengthening of local councils' planning controls, in 1947, village form has lain very much in the hands of local councils, but they have responded in different ways to proposals for new buildings in the villages of West Yorkshire. A tight grip has been held on the growth of Tong. The rejection of proposals for new buildings in the green belt have played a key part in maintaining Tong's linear form. Nevertheless, since 1978, some proposals to build new houses have been approved when these filled in gaps between existing buildings along Tong Lane or when they rounded off the village. Within the latter framework, the 1987-88 proposals to build houses at Hill Green Farm were recommended for approval, as it was believed new houses would improve the appearance of a site then occupied by a large slurry pit and farm buildings in varying states of decay.

Twentieth century growth has resulted in many villages acquiring compact forms, albeit of large sizes. One such village is East Keswick. By the mid-nineteenth century, a branched form was apparent and, a century later, this had become pronounced (Figure 9.1 b). Right at the beginning of the twentieth century, East Keswick had acquired a southwards extension when houses were erected to accommodate employees of Mr Moon, an East Keswick grocer. During the inter-war period, a northern branch of the village was extended by the erection of a line of semi-detached houses. After the Second World War, the village was ear-marked for commuter growth by its proximity to Leeds, where service industries were rapidly expanding, and by an

Figure 9.2. East Bierley: a branched village with a green.

increase in car ownership. East Keswick's pleasant appearance and its setting within a farmed area were equally important attractions. Furthermore, some East Keswick landowners were prepared to sell land to builders, and, despite existing residents' objection, local and national governments supported some growth in the 1960s. In itself, this went a considerable way towards changing East Keswick into a compact village, and the transformation was completed by a second phase of growth in the 1970s. Infilling between existing branches has thus created East Keswick's compact form. With so many different phases of growth in the village, many different house styles occur which include old darkened stone houses with flagged roofs, inter-war semi-detached brick houses and post-war detached houses some of which are stone built with slate roofs.

Many villages possess a green which may be small, like that at Lower Cumberworth, or large, such as the one at Sharlston. The green at Thorner, which replaced fields and a railway line, and the green at Oxenhope, which was developed to celebrate the millennium, are both recent features, but many greens existed prior to the twentieth century. In the eighteenth century, the village of Notton comprised a slightly winding row of buildings in the west and buildings surrounding a large green in the east. The green part of the village might have been deliberately planned, but if this is so, it is very different from the rectangular village greens of North Yorkshire which are believed to have been planned in medieval times. So despite its large size, the green at Notton may be just one of several that appear to have arisen more by accident than design. This is certainly the case in East Bierley which is today located at a road junction, as it was in 1775. In that year a small patch of open land was trapped between the two roads, but buildings were erected only along parts of the western road. During the nineteenth century, the village extended northwards from the junction, and in the inter-war period houses were built along the road south of the junction. Consequently, by 1939, the open land of 1775 had become a green at the centre of the village (Figure 9.2).

FIELD BOUNDARIES

Of West Yorkshire's contemporary field boundaries, the oldest, albeit flanked by recently erected barbed wire fences, might well be that which runs for half a kilometre just to the west of Bullerthorpe Lane, Colton. This boundary is part of Grim's Ditch which is believed to have originated as a territorial boundary in the Iron Age (Figure 3.2 and chapter three). Almost as rare, but not so old, are those narrow, elongated, slightly curved fields, best seen near Clifton, Brighouse, which might be fossilised medieval strips (Figure 9.3a). Most West Yorkshire field patterns, though, are of two kinds. Irregular sized and shaped fields characterise many parts of central West Yorkshire and certain places in the eastern lowlands, but elsewhere straight, regular shaped fields predominate (Figure 4.6 and 9.3b). In a few small areas, such as to the south east of Temple Newsam, near Leeds, and immediately to the north west of Anglers Country Park, near Wakefield, straight edged fields have been very recently formed by the restoration of open cast mining sites. However, most regular shaped fields were laid out when common or waste was enclosed by Act of Parliament (chapter four). Since then, although the boundaries remain straight, the size of many fields have changed. At Emley Moor the pattern broadly resembles that of 1842, when the area had not long been enclosed, but in detail some fields have been enlarged and others sub-divided.

(a)

(b)

Figure 9.3. Contemporary (a) elongated fields near Clifton; (b) irregular fields, Shibden Dale.

Nor is change restricted to field patterns formed by parliamentary enclosure. Many of the elongated fields that existed at Clifton, in 1788, have been converted into other shapes, and of the few elongated fields that remain today, scarcely one is exactly as it was in 1788. Given this magnitude of change over two centuries, and the absence of medieval maps of fields, it is far from certain, how many, if any, of the field shapes at Clifton are fully the same as in medieval times. Similar uncertainty relates to the fields with irregular shapes. It is conceivable that these field patterns are largely inherited from medieval assarts, but even when, as in parts of Shibden Dale, it is highly likely that the fields originated in this way, the links between contemporary field shapes and assarts have yet to be established. In Shibden Dale the issue is further clouded

by a change from hedgerow boundaries to stone walls. This change may have occurred during the seventeenth and eighteenth centuries, and it is possible that, at the same time, some of the field shapes were also changed.

Within the last forty years, as the recreational activity of horse riding has increased in popularity, some West Yorkshire fields have been sub-divided by wooden fences to produce small grazing areas for horses. Nevertheless, stone walls still characterise field boundaries in the Pennines, just as hedges continue to be typical of those boundaries which remain in the eastern lowlands. There, though, large numbers of hedges have been uprooted to create truly enormous fields (Figure 9.4). These not only make it easier for farmers to use large ploughs and harvesters, but also enable them to readily

Figure 9.4. A huge field of recently harvested wheat, Methley.

change the proportions of either different crops grown or land set aside from year to year.

RECENT CHANGES IN CROPS AND LIVESTOCK

By the early nineties, contrasts in the farmed landscape had become sharper than in the mid-sixties in an area lying approximately between the Wharfe and the Calder and east of Bradford. In the eastern Pennines, north of the Calder, the area under grass increased while that of crops, especially vegetables, declined. Conversely in the arable east, the grassland area declined, as more and more grass was ploughed up for crops, especially cereals and oil seed rape. Some of the increase in the cereal and oil seed rape area was also at the expense of vegetables.

Whilst the area under vegetables, in West Yorkshire, has continued to decline, new trends have emerged during the last decade. Although sheep numbers have more or less held their own, cattle numbers have declined, and that despite an increase in the number of beef cattle. Dairy cattle have become far less numerous since the European Union introduced milk quotas as part of their attempt to reduce European food output. Moreover, to be viable, some dairy farmers would have had to expand, but that would have involved a level of investment beyond their means, so such farmers changed from dairying to other livestock farming.

During the 1990s the area under maize increased, though its total area remains small. The increase has occurred because certain farmers have recognised the value of maize both as a mixed livestock feed and as an additional feed when weather conditions make grass less available. In addition, maize was grown in 2002 near Oglethorpe Hills, Bramham, as part of genetically modified crop trials (Figure 9.5).

In 1992 the European Union strengthened its resolve to reduce the growth of cereals by reducing its price support for cereals. Farmers were compensated by Arable Area Payments, but a farmer receives these payments only when that farmer takes some land out of cultivation. The scheme is not compulsory, but as most of West Yorkshire's cereal farmers have decided to seek payments, so set-aside has partly replaced cereals. Individual West Yorkshire farmers select the type of set-aside best suited to their needs. They either leave autumn stubble in the ground for almost a year, or leave a margin of grass around a field that is otherwise growing crops (Figure 9.6). Only rarely do farmers use set-aside fields to grow a crop mixture that will not be harvested, but will provide food for wild birds. Although Arable Area Payments include certain other crops grown for food such as oil seed rape, the latter has not experienced the same decline in area as cereals, because it is also grown for industrial use. Nevertheless, oil seed rape still occupies a far smaller area than cereals.

Outside a contemporary market gardening core centred upon Carlton (near Rothwell), the area occupied by fruit and vegetables has declined since the seventies. This is particularly noticeable in an area approximately bounded by Calverley, Kirkstall, Ossett and Mirfield where many fields of vegetables, particularly those growing rhubarb, have been replaced by grass or buildings. Of the grass, some is used for recreational activities, some for hobby farming and some is scarcely used. Forced rhubarb is ready for sale in late winter, a time when there is little competition from home grown fruit. Since the seventies, large quantities of fruit have been imported into the UK in winter, with the consequence that the national demand for rhubarb has declined. In itself this led to a decline in rhubarb production, but it also discouraged some of the younger generation from taking over a family rhubarb business, particularly when less physically arduous work, at an equal or better rate of pay, was available.

Figure 9.5. Maize near Oglethorpe Hills.

CONTEMPORARY CROPLAND, GRASSLAND AND MOORLAND

Vegetable growing is now concentrated in an area centred upon Carlton and lying between Leeds and Wakefield (Figure 9.7). Beyond this core, vegetables are grown in several

Note set aside strip at field edge

Figure 9.6. Grass margin set-aside, Aberford.

market gardening, soils continue to be improved by the addition of waste shoddy obtained from West Yorkshire's textile industry. Rhubarb farmers also grow brassicas, as these provide a cash crop when the soil is being rested from rhubarb in order to reduce the risk of disease.

Market gardening in the Carlton area continues to be aided by the area's proximity to the large markets in Leeds and other large towns. This core area is close to the M1 and M62, and so has excellent access to national supermarkets which are an important source of income for rhubarb growers. The decline in rhubarb growing has been stemmed since the late nineties by renewed interest in its health promoting properties, and by the determination of producers, noticeably the Oldroyds, to grow the crop. The Oldroyds have generated interest by opening their sheds to the public when the forced rhubarb is ready for sale. People travel from as far away as Cornwall to participate in this event (Figure 9.9).

Soft fruits are grown in small localised areas near to Altofts, Emley, Garforth, Norwood Green and Roberttown. These places are situated near many town-dwellers who not only provide a market, but, on pick your own farms, effectively provide a cheap labour supply. All but Roberttown are sited far enough away from houses and main roads to reduce theft loss; such a loss led to the ending of strawberry growing at

scattered localities. Within the grassland area is a tiny organic market garden, near Lightcliffe, but too small to be shown on the land use map (Figure 9.7). Vegetables are grown on the outskirts of Wakefield near Bottom Boat, Chevet Grange and Kettlethorpe. Potatoes are grown in a few fields on the large crop farms in the eastern lowlands, and a small area of rhubarb in still to be found west of Leeds (Figure 9.8). The rhubarb grown at Farsley is sold to Bradford Market which is only a short distance away. Both at Farsley and in the core area for

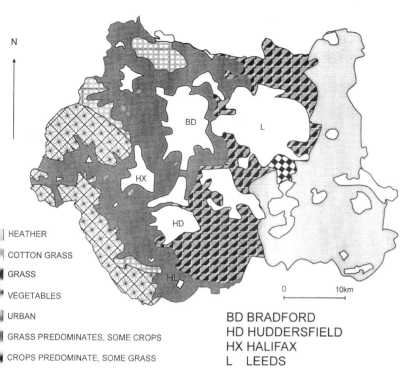

N

HEATHER

COTTON GRASS

GRASS

VEGETABLES

URBAN

GRASS PREDOMINATES, SOME CROPS

CROPS PREDOMINATE, SOME GRASS

0   10km

BD BRADFORD
HD HUDDERSFIELD
HX HALIFAX
L   LEEDS

Figure 9.7. Major Land Use Regions in West Yorkshire.

Figure 9.8. Mr Procter lifts rhubarb roots before replanting them in a forcing shed at Farsley.

Roundhay. Grapes are successfully grown for wine making at Leaventhorpe, as the area is situated within the warmest part of West Yorkshire and is sited on well drained soils. The site faces south, and so has the crucial extra autumnal sunshine that promotes the accumulation of sugars in the grapes.

Most of the improved farmland is occupied by cereals and other crops in the eastern lowlands, but by grass in the west (Figures 9.4, 9.7, 9.10). This contrast is strongly influenced by rainfall. Cereals predominate in the east where the mean annual rainfall is under 700 millimetres, whereas grass predominates in the wetter west. This relationship arises because farmers seek high incomes. Other things being equal, incomes are higher when yields are higher. But yields are, in turn, influenced by rainfall. Cereal yields are greater than those of grass in the drier areas, whilst grass yields are higher than cereal yields in the wetter west. Hence, cereals predominate in the drier east; grass in the west. Black plastic bags containing silage (Figure 2.8) are now a frequent sight on many grassland

Figure 9.9. Mrs Oldroyd-Hulme lights the inside of a rhubarb shed at Carlton.

of which contribute to the total area of grass. Some land is also under grass as set-aside. Furthermore, several cropland farmers also keep livestock, so at least a small area of grassland, where livestock can graze out of doors, is to be found on many eastern lowlands crop farms. Certain farmers in the grassland west grow some cereals to help fatten their beef cattle, though where the mean annual rainfall exceeds about 1,000 millimetres it ceases to be worthwhile to grow cereals. Soil types also influence the relative importance of crops and grass. Within the area where grass predominates but some crops are grown, crops are more significant on brown earths than glei soils, and within the predominantly cropped area, amounts of grass are least on brown calcareous soil. Indeed, on gentle slopes in the extreme south eastern corner of West Yorkshire, an almost Prairie like landscape of huge fields of cereals has developed where brown calcareous soil coincides with the highest summer temperatures and lowest rainfall in the county.

It might come as a surprise that landscapes of the twenty first century should be so influenced by the physical environment. Yet as economic and political constraints are broadly similar throughout West Yorkshire, farmers' decisions are strongly influenced by the county's substantial differences

farms, especially those engaged in dairying. In high rainfall areas, hay is more difficult to make than silage, but silage can offer a fine cattle food. Although the agricultural landscape is so strongly influenced by rainfall, there are other factors that influence its detail.

Localised steep slopes and floodplains are rarely worth ploughing, and so are usually in grass even in the eastern lowlands. Within this region, there are numerous parks, parts in relief, rainfall and soils. Some features, though, elude explanation. There appears to be no reason why crop growing ceases when mean annual rainfall exceeds about 780 millimetres in the north, but about 1,000 millimetres in the south. Nor is it clear why some areas have been left as moorland with a current mean annual rainfall of 900 millimetres, whilst in other cases, areas have been reclaimed with a current rainfall of 1,400 millimetres. Although moorland limits are not easily accounted for, it can at least be said that

Figure 9.10. Grassland farming near Honley.

Figure 9.11. Cotton grass moor, Rishworth; looking towards Baitings Reservoir.

large patches of moorland still exist more because of their value for outdoor recreation and their perceived beauty than for their use for grazing sheep.

The northern moors are characterised by large areas of heather, whilst the southern moors consist of large areas of cotton grass (Figures 9.7, 9.11, 9.12). Whilst both communities are associated with gentle slopes, cotton grass - a sedge or grass like plant - grows on thick beds of peat, whereas heather thrives best in better drained areas. However, it is

Figure 9.12. Controlled heather burning, Burley Moor.

Marsden Moor Estate. From time to time, bales of heather are dropped from a helicopter on to parts of the moor. Volunteers then collect pieces of this heather and scatter the seeds across the peat.

WOODLAND

West Yorkshire is peppered with small patches of woodland some of which have been created within the last thirty years or so. Two recently planted woodlands have replaced moorland on Rombalds Moor to the east of Silsden and to the south of Hades, near Holmfirth. The successful growth of trees at both sites strengthens the claim that West Yorkshire's moorlands exist only because of human activity. Small woods now occupy a former colliery site at Woodlesford, and trees have recently been planted on the former Walton colliery site, near Wakefield.

regular controlled burning, between October and March, that is crucial in maintaining heather moors (Figure 9.12). Burning prevents less fire resistant plants from competing with heather, and it destroys old stems and so promotes the growth of young shoots. But burning has to be controlled, otherwise the whole plant would be destroyed and with it the organic matter in the soil. A new method of developing a cover of heather is used on parts of the National Trust's

In fact throughout West Yorkshire, minute patches of trees have been recently planted. Leeds Countryside Unit has planted trees in a field at Ouzelwell Green whilst near Toil's Farm, Eldwick, one privately owned field has been completely planted with trees which, in time, should become a small wood.

Coniferous woodlands can occur at any height, but woodlands of non-coniferous trees, such as oak and elm, are virtually restricted to altitudes below about 300 metres. Many

West Yorkshire woods are a mixed assemblage of coniferous and non-coniferous trees. An area of woodland has existed in the upper Dearne valley since medieval times. Down the centuries this Upper Dearne Wood has had different owners who, whilst carefully managing the wood, have each introduced different species thereby creating the mixed wood found today.

The small plantation recently established near Toil's Farm has a quadrilateral shape set by the shape of the field in which the trees have been planted. In contrast, the indented oval shape of the woodland surrounding Eccup Reservoir faithfully follows the shape of that reservoir. The shape of some of the woodland boundaries at both Ogden and Mixenden Reservoirs reflects pre-existing trackways, but each of their western boundaries is completely straight and unrelated to other features. The 2.5 kilometres eastern boundary of Rombald's Moor Plantation also lies indifferent to other features, including the relief of the land. Such straight boundaries are often found in twentieth century plantations where the area to be planted has been planned. Older woodland often has patterns which relate to slope gradient. Linear patterns frequently occur on scarps, including Woolley Edge, where the slopes are so steep they could not be easily or cheaply built upon and cultivated, and so have been left wooded. When steep gradients occur along the sides of a main valley and its tributaries, woodland takes a branched pattern. The valleys which converge upon Hebden Bridge offer an especially fine illustration of such a sinuous pattern of woodland.

Some Sources and Further Reading

So little has apparently been written, as articles or books, on this chapter's themes that I have had to make great use of **primary sources** which have included the following.

Maps including Thomas Jefferys (The County of York Survey'd) 1775, and various editions of large scale Ordnance Survey Maps.

The 1:25,000 Land Use maps of West Yorkshire that were published in the 1960s (Large parts of the county were never published).

Extensive field work including mapping contemporary rural land use.

Asking people questions.

Agricultural statistics for various years published by DEFRA. Many of these statistics were obtained from the internet.

Information from Bradford Council Planning Office.

Secondary Sources

CRUMP, W. B. *Clifton And Its Common Fields*, Halifax Antiquarian Society, 1925.

East Keswick Millennium Book, written and published by East Keswick Millennium Group, 2000.

GRIGG, D. *An Introduction to Agricultural Geography*, Hutchinson, 1984.

MACDONALD, A. S. *Tong Hall*, published by the author and Tercentenary Committee, 2002.

SILSON, A. *The scenery of set-aside*, Geographical, March 1995.

Places to Visit

The villages of **East Keswick, Tong** and one of: **Notton, East Bierley, Sharlston.** You might wish to compare the growth and form of a village near your home with one of these villages.

Walk from Saltaire to Ilkley via Dick Hudson's. One of the finest of West Yorkshire's walks will enable you to observe great contrasts in rural land use, and, in summer, will bring the sight and smell of flowering heather.

Follow the footpaths in part of the **eastern arable lands** and observe the crops, farmhouses and fields.

Oldroyd's rhubarb sheds, **Carlton,** are for a very brief period, open to the public by prior booking at Wakefield Council Tourist Office.

Urban Farms are open to the public at several locations including **Crigglestone, Meanwood** and **Temple Newsam.**

PARKS AND GARDENS

WEST YORKSHIRE'S PARKS and gardens possess great variety, but they have in common the presence of shrubs or trees. Nor is the significance of trees merely a present-day phenomena: the earliest known parks were woodlands in which deer roamed.

DEER PARKS

Medieval deer parks, such as those at Pontefract and Roundhay, were established so that the nobility could enjoy either the thrill of the chase or fire arrows at fleeing deer and, as a bonus, delight in the taste of venison. Deer from Sandal Park and perhaps from Old Park, Stanley, and New Park, Ossett, were an important source of food for Sandal Castle. As deer herds thrive in woodland, a deer park was made by surrounding a large patch of woodland with either a ditch or an embankment and pale which kept the herds within the enclosure.

Roundhay ceased to be a deer park when almost all the park's trees had been felled for timber. The cleared area was then divided into fields and farmed. Part of the former deer park re-emerged as a park in the early nineteenth century (chapter one). A three metre deep ditch is reported to occur on private land near Roundhay Grange Farm and is believed to be part of the former deer park boundary. Hall Park, a formerly detached part of Thorp Arch, is partly surrounded by an embankment, up to two metres high, which once probably prevented deer from straying from the park. Despite such features, the direct effects of former deer parks on the landscape are small. Indirectly they were the forerunners of modern parks, as they established the principle that land could be ear-marked for recreational activities.

Lotherton Park was given to Leeds Council in 1968. Deer were introduced, as a visitor attraction, into part of the existing park about twenty years ago, and there is now a large herd (Figure 10.1). Indeed the number of deer has increased so quickly that some are sold to a butcher who then sells the venison and some are sent to re-stock other deer parks including one near South Milford in North Yorkshire. When Lister Park, Bradford, and Bretton Country Park were privately owned, each park included a deer park within its perimeter. However, it seems likely that, like modern day Lotherton, deer occupied existing parkland rather than, as in medieval times, parkland specifically created for deer.

Figure 10.1. A parkland, of grass with scattered trees, occupied by deer in 2002, Lotherton. Margaret Plows.

COUNTRY HOUSE PARKS

Whereas most of West Yorkshire's human landscapes are a product of wealth production, parks arose from wealth disposal. It became fashionable in the eighteenth and nineteenth centuries for a person of means to set his imposing residence amongst an equally tasteful park. Substantial wealth was required to build and maintain a park and allow the park's owner sufficient free time to admire his achievement. Moreover, the park was not only intended to provide personal satisfaction, but to be flaunted in front of a wider selection of the leisured class. In the later nineteenth century, the newly affluent manufacturers emulated their social betters by living in large houses surrounded by parks and gardens.

Robert Benson, a wealthy lawyer's son, began to empark part of Bramham Moor in 1698. Apart from a house, Bramham Park soon acquired three components which are retained today. There is a large area of grass and scattered trees with an avenue leading to the house, a woodland pleasure grounds dissected by intersecting, straight rides and there is a garden most of which is a formal type found nowhere else in West Yorkshire (Figure 10.2). The formal garden consists of long, straight, intersecting stretches of grass bounded by beech hedges up to eight metres tall. At one intersection a branched, straight sided canal is to be seen. This maze like landscape is of a French style that was deliberately designed to be revealed only gradually to an observer. Even as the canal was being constructed in the 1730s, ideas on beauty were changing, and were already

Figure 10.2. Bramham Park Garden. This photograph has been included by permission of Bramham Park Estate.

finding expression at Nostell Priory when its lake was given curved edges.

Lancelot 'Capability' Brown was an eighteenth century landscape gardener who believed beauty resided in curvaceous lakes and belts of woodland, and in clumps of trees set amongst large areas of grass. He believed the landscape garden should have a more natural appearance than that of the

Figure 10.3. Bretton Country Park. This illustration, which includes a sculpture by Henry Moore, has been included by permission of the Henry Moore Foundation.

Newsam Park, Leeds, but the Yorkshire Sculpture Park, when it opened in 1977, was Great Britain's only formally designated sculpture park. As such, it is well placed by the M1 and attracts visitors from within and from without, West Yorkshire.

Within West Yorkshire, Brown himself influenced the landscapes at Temple Newsam, Whitley Park and Harewood. At the latter, the two adjacent estates of Harewood and Gawthorpe were to be remarkably transformed in the eighteenth century. In 1739 Henry Lascelles and his son, Edwin, took up residence in the Old Hall, Gawthorpe which was then set amongst a deer park and a formal garden. The remainder of their Gawthorpe estate, along with that of Harewood, was occupied partly by woodland, but principally by enclosed farmland. In 1753 the estates passed to Edwin who expended enormous effort in replacing the Old Hall with a much grander house which was set within a visually improved landscape. This was achieved by removing field boundaries from a central area which then became a large park of grassland with scattered trees. A central woodland belt was also cleared, but large numbers of trees were planted in the west where a valley was dammed to form a large, curved and branched lake. A 'Capability' Brown landscape had been created which substantially remains today.

Within the branches of the lake, a large kitchen garden provided the household with fresh fruit, vegetables and cut

formal garden. For much of the eighteenth, and into the nineteenth century, Brown's tenets held sway either through his own work or that of his followers.

Bretton Park was 'landscaped' in accord with Brown's principles in the eighteenth century. Today most of the park is either the Yorkshire Sculpture Park where its grass is mown or Bretton Country Park where its rough grass is grazed by sheep. Pieces of sculpture adorn both parks (Figure 10.3). Fifty years ago some of Henry Moore's work was exhibited in Temple

flowers. Heat was trapped within the garden by surrounding brick walls. Here the head gardener would nurture crops in a very labour intensive manner in environments that ranged from hot glasshouses on the south facing wall to the cooler conditions of the north facing wall. Today, the presence of brick walls in the gardens of country houses often indicates a former kitchen garden, even where a such a garden no longer exists.

About the end of the eighteenth century, there was renewed debate on beauty in the landscape. Brown's landscapes were considered by some to be rather monotonous, rather sparse and insufficiently natural. These advocates of the picturesque believed in a wilder appearance, a more densely clothed landscape and in a degree of apparent neglect, so they favoured the presence of ruins or follies designed to appear ancient.

Early in the nineteenth century, another belt of land was incorporated into Harewood's grounds thereby adding a ready-made picturesque landscape of woodland and an actual ruined castle. The mid-nineteenth century witnessed some return to formality at Harewood, when two terraces and a parterre were added to the front of the house. Since the 1950s, fees from visitors have contributed to the maintenance of the estate and in order to encourage visitors, a children's area and a bird garden have been built. In 1993 the parterre was restored by agricultural students using English Heritage and European Community funds.

The picturesque is taken to its limits in the landscape gardens at St Ives, Harden. In the nineteenth century, the estate was owned by the Ferrand family who created a large lake, planted trees and incorporated an area of heather as a heather park. The garden's wild appearance is accentuated by occasional bare rock outcrops such as Lady Blantyre's Rock. St Ives Park is now owned by Bradford Council.

MUNICIPAL PARKS 1850 TO 1980

Until the mid-nineteenth century, West Yorkshire's parks were developed for the pleasure of an affluent resident owner and his immediate circle. For centuries, members of the lower order had used commons for outdoor recreation. As an example, knurr and spell and bowling using stones were frequent pastimes in the early nineteenth century on Baildon Moor. By 1850 much common had been enclosed, though some remains even today including that at Baildon Moor and South Hiendley which are each used for outdoor recreation. However, by 1850 a paucity of public transport and rapid urban expansion had left many town dwellers far removed from public open spaces.

Sir Francis Crossley, a wealthy carpet manufacturer, remedied this state of affairs for the urban dwellers of Halifax by creating The People's Park which opened in 1857 (Figure 10.4). During a visit to New Hampshire, USA, Crossley had experienced an almost spiritual vision of its landscapes. Consequently, on his return to England, he resolved to create, in Halifax, a beautiful landscape which might enable its people to enjoy an experience resembling his own. The park was built by Crossley's own house for, in return for his costly venture, he hoped to obtain pleasure from observing people enjoy his beautiful park. Halifax Corporation was as far-sighted as Crossley, for it accepted responsibility for the park's upkeep, a cost that was only partly off-set by an endowment which Crossley later gave to the Corporation.

Few indeed were prepared to follow completely in Crossley's footsteps, though there were several who gave land, on which parks were to be made, to local councils. Even profit making amusement parks were rare, both in time and space. Sunny Vale Gardens, Hipperholme, opened in 1880 and thirteen years later, Hope Bank Pleasure Gardens opened at Honley. Both gardens

Figure 10.4. The People's Park, Halifax, September 2002. The speaker is Lord Somerleyton, a direct descendent of Francis Crossley, and the ceremony is to mark the restoration of the park.

public parks was becoming so accepted that the enclosure of Wibsey and Low Moor commons was agreed only on condition that parts of the commons became public parks. As a result, Wibsey Park and Harold Park both opened in 1885. After 1862 many private parks were acquired by local councils thereby preventing the parks from falling into decay. Thus, Peel Park - which had been created by a group of Bradford residents following a public meeting in 1850 - was conveyed to Bradford Corporation in 1863. Even more crucially, by making their own parks, and by acquiring existing parks, local councils have kept land open that might otherwise have fallen to builders.

Nineteenth century councillors, who sought to have public parks provided, probably wanted residents of densely built up areas to be able to appreciate the sight of grass, trees and perhaps lakes, within short distances of their homes. Councillors' aims widened in the early twentieth century when many believed that parks should enable people to become fitter. In the 1920s, South Kirkby Council decided a park was needed for children's play during the long school holidays.

included a lake and, at Hope Bank, a steam boat ride on the lake was an attraction. Hope Bank's other attractions included swings, switchback rides and donkey rides. Both amusement parks were still in business in the inter-war period, but an amusement park at Golden Acre, Bramhope, lasted only from 1932-38. In the second half of the nineteenth century, with so little private investment, it accordingly fell to local councils to provide public parks. Moreover, the 1860 Public Improvement Act at last enabled local authorities to use rates to acquire and maintain public parks. By 1880 recognition of the need for

It might be expected that as a result of these various purposes, each park would have developed a variety of landscapes. This is by no means always the case, and often a particular landscape predominates. So at Centre Vale Park, Todmorden, substantial provision for outdoor games leads to a predominance of playing fields. In contrast, The People's Park at Halifax, which lately has been restored to its nineteenth century glory, remains an island of beauty, lacking provision for playing active games (Figure 10.4).

Beaumont Park, Huddersfield, is as wild as parks come in West Yorkshire. It is predominantly wooded, consisting mostly of deciduous trees but with some evergreens, and shrubs such as rhododendrons and holly. Bare rock outcrops, which in some places reach heights of about fifteen metres, accentuate the wildness (Figure 10.5). Yet within the same town, and opening only one year after Beaumont, Greenhead Park is, today, utterly different. Greenhead Park is best categorised as a public amusement park as so much of its landscape is occupied by bowling greens, tennis courts, skate board rides, a children's paddling pool, a bandstand and a stage. There is a fine miniature railway too. Beaumont is so different from Greenhead partly because it is further from the city centre and so less accessible, but mainly because it occupies a very different site. Greenhead lies on gentle slopes which have made it easy for the park to be adapted to changing purposes. Beaumont occupies a landslip which has formed the steep rock back wall and the slightly hummocky ground at its base. This difficult terrain was already well wooded when it was acquired in 1883 by the Council, which sensibly decided it would be too difficult and too expensive to modify.

Figure 10.5. Beaumont Park, Huddersfield.

Many formerly privately owned parks retain their predominance of grass and scattered trees because they are now used as golf courses. Examples include Crow Nest, Brighouse, and Gott's, Armley. However, the predominantly grass and scattered tree parkland obtained by Bradford Council from SC Lister, has been greatly transformed. The first major change involved making a large lake, later to be used for boating. Cartwright Hall was erected in Lister Park between 1900-04, and, at that time, a formal flower bed was laid in front of the hall. Between 1912-25 an outdoor Swimming Pool, now filled in, a bowling green and tennis courts were added. When Leeds Council acquired Roundhay Park, lakes already existed which were later used for boating. As at Lister Park, a bowling green and tennis courts were added, and for a time there was an outdoor swimming pool. However, as Roundhay Park is much larger than Lister Park, a much larger amount of parkland of grass and scattered trees remains at Roundhay.

Since 1999, new gardens have been made at Roundhay Park and Lister Park. Roundhay has a Monet Garden and a beautiful

Figure 10.6. Mughul Garden, Lister Park, Bradford.

Alhambra Garden. It was intended that these two gardens would be part of Seven Gardens of the World, but insufficient funds have stalled the project. At Lister Park, the Mughul Garden opened in 2001 (Figure 10.6). The garden's design incorporates features from India and Pakistan, and was created to reflect the high proportion of Asians resident in Bradford and, in particular in Manningham, where the park is located.

DOMESTIC GARDENS

During the nineteenth century, existing town gardens very often succumbed to building, and most new houses were built with no, or only small, gardens. As a result, allotment gardens were established to offer the working man an alternative or additional form of physical recreation to playing games. They were a quiet urban oasis over which the working man had a measure of control that was absent from mine or factory work. The vegetables produced also helped to provide a balanced diet, and occasionally supplemented the income when vegetables were sold for a few pence to neighbours. Though fewer allotments exist today, those which remain not only continue to offer most valuable recreation, but can be cultivated for organic vegetables at a cost that is lower than prices in retail outlets. Some families believe organic vegetables keep their children in good health, and it is this concern that has partly led to the renewal of interest in allotment keeping within the last decade. Allotments continue to possess a distinctive landscape because a given allotment consists of small plots which are rented to individuals who each cultivate their flowers and vegetables in their own way.

Since 1950, a multitude of new domestic gardens have compensated for a decline in the area occupied by allotments. The landscapes of small suburban and commuter village gardens are, like those of allotments, a matter of individual taste. This, though, is influenced by a variety of factors including fashion, and, within the last decade, the public opening of relatively small private gardens. They may be open for only a day or two a year, perhaps to raise funds for a charity, but they act as an incentive and a source of ideas for the amateur gardener.

PARKS AND NATURE RESERVES ESTABLISHED SINCE 1980

Many new parks and nature reserves have been developed on former industrial sites. Some farms, including a market garden at Drighlington, have been converted to golf courses. Two worked out open cast sites at Pugneys and Anglers (both to the south of Wakefield), instead of being restored to farming, were converted into country parks, and opened in the mid-1980s. As this is being written, work is proceeding to convert St Aidan's open cast mine into a huge park-cum-nature reserve. The virtual ending of deep coal mining in West Yorkshire has left, in its wake, large derelict sites which have not always proven popular for new industrial activity, and some have been acquired by local authorities to provide new country parks. Rothwell Country Park, which opened in 2000 on the site of Rothwell Colliery, is an excellent example. The colliery closed in 1983 and the site lay derelict until 1995 when Leeds City Council and Ground Work Leeds, aided by the community and using funds from a variety of sources, began to convert the site into a park. This large park has a raw appearance as its trees are immature, and improved grass is all but absent. Some features of the previous landscape, including old railway lines, have been deliberately retained. Walton Colliery Nature Park, Wakefield, is just as bleak.

The demolition of Kirkstall and Skelton Grange thermal power stations has provided sites for nature reserves. That at

Figure 10.7. Horton Bank Top Country Park.

which has been converted into a country park (Figure 10.7). Although most of the water has been drained, a lake still exists in a basin backed by steep bare rock. Grass is sparse, but there are numerous young trees. Most of Rodley Sewage Works has been converted into a nature reserve by volunteers who have leased the land from Yorkshire Water. Part of the nature reserve has also replaced fields where once cereals and vegetables grew. A mixed landscape of marsh, lake, wet grassland, scrub and coppice woodland has been made. The latter was, for a very short period, cut to generate environmentally friendly electricity at a North Yorkshire power station.

Not all new parks and nature reserves are sited on derelict industrial sites. A chemical business called Zeneca, in a joint venture with Kirklees Countryside Unit, developed land near Dalton chemical works into a vast nature reserve which opened to the public in 1991. The reserve was designed to provide a great variety of wildlife habitats, but, as its main attributes are grassland and a large wooded area, it has effectively provided Huddersfield with a new large park.

Kirkstall so closely resembles Rothwell Country Park that it might as readily be called a park as a nature reserve. Just as small power stations closed when the national electricity grid was improved, so recent improvements in the long distance movement of water have led to the closure of a few small reservoirs. One such closure has been Horton Bank Top Reservoir

Some Sources and Further Reading

BENTLEY, J. *Illustrated Handbook of the Bradford City Parks,* Bradford Corporation, 1926.

BURT, S. *An Illustrated History of Roundhay Park,* Burt S, n/d.

LEEDS CITY COUNCIL *The opening of Rothwell Country Park,* 2000.

MAUCHLINE, M. *Harewood House,* MPC, 1992.

McCRAKEN, S. *Bramham Park,* No publisher, n/d.

POWELL, K. People's Inheritance, Metropolitan Borough of Calderdale, 1984.

SKELTON, T. *Leeds' golden acres,* Age Concern, 2000.

SHEERAN, G. *Landscape Gardens In West Yorkshire, 1680-1880,* Wakefield Historical Publications, 1990.

Places to Visit

Your local park may be visited to identify which of the landscapes and processes described in this chapter can be identified.

Any of the parks mentioned in this chapter are well worth a visit, but representatives of the different park and garden landscapes are visible at the following parks.

Anglers Country Park, Wintersett. Nearby is the Waterton Countryside Discovery Centre.

Beaumont, Huddersfield.

Bramham.

Bretton.

Greenhead, Huddersfield.

Harewood.

Lister, Bradford.

Roundhay, Leeds.

Rothwell Country Park.

The People's, Halifax.

In West Leeds a variety of different parks and gardens can be appreciated on a walk that takes in Kirkstall Wild Flower Garden, Kirkstall Nature Reserve, Gott's Park, Armley and Armley Park.

CASTLES AND OTHER FORTIFICATIONS

THE VIEW NORTH east from Kettlethorpe is eye catching. A conical hill, for all the world resembling an ash volcano, can be seen rising above the surface of a distant ridge. The hill is, in fact, a motte, a man-made mound of earth that was constructed as a part of a twelfth century castle at Sandal. Mottes and the baileys (courtyards) which lie alongside them were medieval features, but ditches and embankments built for defence have a far longer time span.

IRON AGE FORTIFICATIONS

Three Iron Age forts have been identified in West Yorkshire at Barwick in Elmet, South Kirkby and on Castle Hill,

Almondbury. The fortifications at Almondbury are now scarcely visible, but they have influenced medieval earthworks which remain part of the landscape. Initially, an embankment was constructed on the south western part of Castle Hill summit, but then, between the early sixth century BC and the mid-fifth century BC, the whole summit was fortified by both banks and ditches. The fort came to an abrupt end, at the close of the fifth century BC, when its timber supports self-ignited.

The Iron Age fort at Barwick in Elmet is sited on Tower Hill and Wendel Hill. That part of the fort located on Wendel Hill is, even today, a most impressive feature. The site on Wendel

Figure 11.1. *(a) The Ridge. (b) A field sketch section of the earthworks at Becca Banks.*

(a)

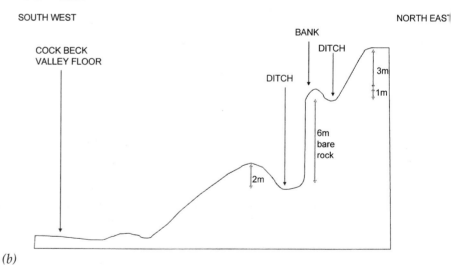

(b)

(Not true to scale)

Hill was well chosen as a capping of Magnesian Limestone has contributed to the formation of a naturally steep north west facing valley side. Near its summit, this slope was further steepened by Iron Age inhabitants who made an almost vertical bank about three metres high. On the eastern side of Wendel Hill, where there was far less natural protection, a combined ditch and bank, which is currently about two metres deep on the outer side and approximately five metres high on the inner side, were constructed.

It seems likely that the Barwick in Elmet hill fort was part of a series of linear earthworks known now as The Ridge and Becca Banks which run from Barwick in Elmet to Aberford. The Ridge comprises a northern three metre high bank immediately followed southwards by a ditch one metre wide and three metres deep (Figure 11.1a). The earthworks at Becca Banks show how their builders possessed a remarkable eye for countryside. The bank is sited immediately above a very steep bare rock valley side. and the ditch is placed where this free face gives way to the valley floor (Figure 11.1b). Twenty years ago, it was believed that these earthworks were constructed in sub-Roman times in order to help defend the Kingdom of Elmet from the Anglo-Saxons. Now, they are thought to have been constructed in the Iron Age, though they may have been re-used in later periods. This revised date for the earthworks has led to the resurrection of a 1950s theory that the earthworks were made to protect the British from Roman invaders.

The Romans built three forts in West Yorkshire (chapter three). Each of the forts had a rectangular plan, but none of the forts is part of the contemporary landscape. Hence, after the Iron Age, there appears to be no landscape evidence of new defensive works being constructed until Late Anglo-Saxon times.

An earthwork with a circular plan is known as a ringwork. That near Kippax Church has a diameter of between twenty-four and thirty-two metres and an embanked perimeter. Kippax ringwork was an administrative stronghold shortly after the Norman Conquest, when a bailey, now a graveyard, existed adjacent to the ringwork. However, the Normans may merely have occupied a ringwork that existed in Late Anglo-Saxon times when Kippax was a centre of a multiple estate (chapter three). At Mirfield there appears to have been a ringwork which might have protected a Late Anglo-Saxon house. It is difficult to be certain because a castle was built upon the site about 1100.

MEDIEVAL EARTHWORK CASTLES

The motte and bailey originated in France, and were introduced into West Yorkshire c.1086 when Ilbert de Lacy built Pontefract Castle. In 1106 the second Earl de Warenne was granted the Manor of Wakefield, and it was probably he who then built Sandal Castle, with the likely expectation that it would provide a secure home on the occasions when he resided in Wakefield. The castle was also a tax gathering centre. Today, Sandal Castle clearly retains the main features of a motte and bailey castle (Figure 11.2).

In the twelfth century, a deep ditch was dug, not only to be a line of defence, but to provide the earth to construct the motte. Some of the earth loosened by digging the ditch was laid and then levelled to form the surface of the bailey. Wooden buildings were erected on the bailey to house the Earl's garrison and servants and, when in Wakefield, the Earl. Were the castle to be attacked, the Earl would have moved to a timber building on the motte. Castles of this type could be rapidly erected, but were vulnerable to attack by fire. Consequently, from about 1180, the castle began to be rebuilt in

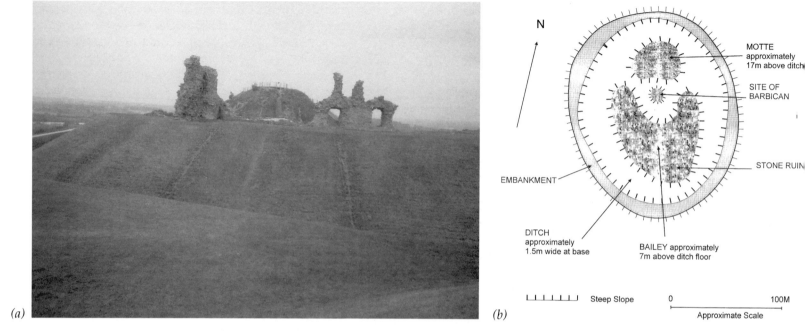

Figure 11.2. *(a) Remains of Sandal Castle from the south. (b) A field sketch map of Sandal Castle today.*

stone, and a stone keep, which was the castle's greatest stronghold, was erected on the motte. By 1250 stone walls, along which were towers to offer extra protection, surrounded the bailey. In 1270 a stone barbican was built to provide extra protection for the keep.

West Yorkshire's other medieval earthwork castles had something in common with Sandal, but there were also differences which may be illustrated from the castles at Pontefract and Almondbury. Pontefract Castle was initially a motte and bailey castle, but by the fifteenth century it had been

strengthened to a greater degree than Sandal by the addition of an upper, outer bailey and a lower, outer bailey to the castle's original inner bailey. Today, though, only the inner bailey can be readily seen. Castle Hill, Almondbury, possessed two baileys, and these, along with a surrounding embankment, are still clearly visible (Figure 11.3). The keep at Castle Hill was built on a ringwork that was largely a medieval modification of an Iron Age ditch. The nineteenth century Victoria Tower now occupies the ringwork.

At least a dozen earthwork castles existed in thirteenth

Figure 11.3. Outer bailey, its embankment and, sited on the inner bailey, a public house and on the ringwork, the Victoria Tower, Castle Hill, Almondbury.

from North Yorkshire. As the functions of castles differed, so too did their locations. The castles at Pontefract and Sandal were both well located from a military stand point. Each castle controlled the important west-east routeway between the Rivers Aire and Calder; Pontefract also lay close to a major north-south road. Both castles were sited upon, or near to, hill tops, which on clear days, provided long distance views that might reveal troop movements. Pontefract Castle had the best site of any West Yorkshire castle for it was perched on top of a steep bare rock outcrop. In the Civil War this proved to be too strong to be mined, hence, explosives could not be laid with the hope of damaging the castle. Tradition claims the site was selected by William I himself. If this is true, he might well have chosen the spot because he saw an Anglo-Saxon earthwork that is believed to have already existed there.

century West Yorkshire, but of these, only Pontefract and Sandal combined important military and administrative functions. Most of the remaining castles were essentially administrative centres, though Bardsey Castle was merely the short-lived home of the Danbys who had been displaced

The sites of some other medieval castles, including Almondbury, Barwick in Elmet, Kippax and Mirfield were

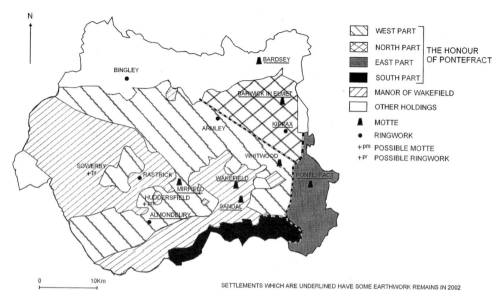

Figure 11.4. *Land Holdings and Earthwork Castles 1166-1400.*

perhaps at Sowerby to administer the Manor's Pennine division. The Honour of Pontefract was divided into four parts, three of which had centres in West Yorkshire. Whilst the East Part was administered by Pontefract, the North Part and the West Part were each administered by lower order centres which, initially, were located at Kippax and Almondbury respectively. In the early thirteenth century, Kippax was largely replaced by Barwick in Elmet where a new motte and bailey castle was built. A century later, this, in turn, seemed to have lost its significance for the castle had become little more than a farm-house. Only slightly earlier, Castle Hill, Almondbury, had become a hunting lodge, and either Bradford or Leeds had taken its place as an administrative centre, though in turn, whichever settlement it was, had been replaced by Rothwell during the fourteenth century.

Other castles probably faired no better, so it is quite likely that by the end of the fourteenth century, the only earthwork castles, though by then rebuilt in stone, to have retained administrative and military significance were those of Pontefract and Sandal. Both of these castles saw action in the Civil War, and when this ended both were deliberately destroyed and fell into ruin. In 2002 only eight earthwork castles appear in West Yorkshire's landscape and of these, Bardsey is little more than a rectangular embanked enclosure, and the Kippax ringwork is more clearly recognised from the

also chosen by the Normans probably because of the presence, at the site, of older defensive earthworks. But the wider locations of earthwork castles, with the exception of Bardsey, were chosen to enable their administrative functions to be easily realised. Most of twelfth century West Yorkshire was divided into two very large tenancies: the Honour of Pontefract held by the de Lacys and the Manor of Wakefield held by the de Warennes (Figure 11.4). As medieval land transport was so poor, it was virtually impossible to administer the whole of the large and oddly shaped Honour of Pontefract from Pontefract or the Manor of Wakefield from Sandal. Accordingly, the Manor of Wakefield possessed subsidiary centres at Rastrick and

air than from the ground. Castle Hill, Almondbury, attracts many visitors, but perhaps more are drawn by the public house opened in 1810 or the Victoria Tower than by the few remains of a medieval ringwork and bailey castle. For some years, local residents have effectively used the remains of Sandal Castle as a small park, but Wakefield Council now seem to be attempting to attract outside visitors as the Council has erected a visitor centre at the castle, and built steps to the

summit of the motte. Pontefract Castle has been a visitor attraction for a much longer period; perhaps people are drawn to the dungeon, and to the inner bailey which became a park in Victorian times.

MEDIEVAL MOATS

Medieval West Yorkshire possessed at least twenty eight moats that were not part of castles, and it is these moats that are the focus of interest in this section. Many medieval moats, including those of East Keswick, Lofthouse and Purston Jaglin, have been accidentally or deliberately destroyed, and, of those which remain, some are only just discernible. One such moat is that at Moat Hall, Scarcroft. Fifty years ago, the Hall was still surrounded by a moat, or at least a ditch, but by the sixties only part remained, and today there is but a thirty centimetres high steepening of the land that was once part of one of the ditch walls. Even in those moats which contain water, many are but a shrunken part of a whole moat. By the mid-nineteenth century, the moat at Scholes (near Barwick in Elmet) had already been cut into two halves by a branch of the Tadcaster to Halton Dial turnpike road, and then, in a late 1930s ribbon growth, the south side of the moat was built upon. A couple of ponds

Figure 11.5. The moat, with a remnant of the Hall on the island, at Thornhill.

are all that now remain of a much larger moat. A minute finger lake is all that is left of a moat at Sturton Grange, Garforth, but at Guiseley, a wide semi-circular lake half surrounds the former rectory. Complete moats occur at Kinsley, Oakwell Hall and Thornhill. The moat at Oakwell Hall is L shaped whereas that at Thornhill completely surrounds an island on which stands a small remnant of Thornhill Hall (Figure 11.5). The Hall was accidentally blown up during the Civil War. Both moats are about five metres wide, though Thornhill moat widens at its south eastern extremity. The enclosure within a rectangular moat at Kinsley is today used to rear ostriches, and the moat has the dual function of keeping people out and preventing the birds from escaping.

However, in medieval times most, perhaps all, enclosures surrounded by a moat contained a building. Those at New Hall, Midgley (near Emley), and Sturton Grange were probably local administrative centres, but most buildings, including that at Roach, Garforth, were probably only houses. Between the thirteenth and fifteenth centuries, when many moats were made, there seems to have existed an upper stratum of society whose members were unable to build a castle because they could neither obtain a licence for a castle nor afford one. They could, though, afford a moat. Therefore, a moat was built as a second best choice. Whilst a moat provided a measure of security against local insurgents and thieves, most moats were probably built to provide a visible sign of the owners' standing and wealth. If this is correct, it could explain why moats were built only in central and eastern West Yorkshire, as these areas were probably wealthier than the extreme west. Within the eastern area, moats were not built where the surface rock is Magnesian Limestone, perhaps because it would have been too expensive to prevent water seeping underground.

Figure 11.6. *The west tower Bolling Hall.*

Medieval and Iron Age fortifications chiefly appear in the contemporary landscape as localised small landforms. But another set of fortifications and castles primarily appear in the landscape as buildings.

FORTIFIED HOUSES AND CASTLES FROM 1366 TO MODERN TIMES

In 1366, when moated properties were still being built in Yorkshire, a castle was built by William de Aldeburgh to be the administrative centre of the Manor of Harewood and to serve as his residence. Harewood Castle was quite different from medieval earthwork castles. It was a single block, solid stone structure built without a bailey. Far more of the castle remains than at either Pontefract or Sandal, but, unfortunately, the building is in a dangerous state.

At a slightly later date, probably in the late fourteenth or early fifteenth centuries, Bolling Hall, Bradford was built by a member of the Bolling family. When it was built, Bolling Hall was a fortified house made up of a castle-like stone tower and one or two adjacent buildings. Most of the existing hall was built after medieval times, but the original tower remains in the extreme west (Figure 11.6). The west tower was a status symbol, but various lines of evidence indicate the tower was also a true fortification. The tower is built on a gentle slope that then falls rapidly to the west, and from this elevated position, there are long distance views down to Bradford and beyond. The tower was built in the turbulent times that culminated in the War of the Roses, and when uprisings by local lords were possible or raids by Scotsmen were a threat. The latter was no imaginary threat for in 1318 almost every house in Knaresborough (North Yorkshire) had been burned down by Scots raiders.

A long period of internal peace followed the Civil War, so existing defensive features fell into decay, and new ones were rarely built. However, in the nineteenth and early twentieth centuries, wealth acquired from the textile industry enabled a number of castles to be built in the Pennines. These castles were large houses which included at least some features of a stone castle, and were primarily designed to visibly proclaim the owner's great wealth and importance. Good examples are Whinburn, Cliffe Castle and Dobroyd Castle. Whinburn, located between Steeton and Keighley, looks remarkably strong with its rectangular northern tower. This house was built in 1897, and was then enlarged and given its fortified appearance between 1912-13 by Sir Prince Prince-Smith who managed the largest textile machine manufacturing business in Europe. As well as displaying his wealth, Prince-Smith may have been seeking to rival Cliffe Castle, Keighley, which had been castellated by the addition of two tall towers between 1874 and 1878. It was Henry Butterfield, an important worsted manufacturer, who was responsible for converting Cliffe Hall into Cliffe Castle. In the mid-nineteenth century, John Fielden was one of three brothers who owned cotton textile mills in Todmorden and district. He had set his heart on marrying a weaver called Ruth Stansfield. The story goes that she would only marry a man who built her a castle. Whether or not this is true, John certainly built the magnificent Dobroyd Castle which occupies a commanding position overlooking the town of Todmorden.

The Second World War introduced new kinds of defensive features into West Yorkshire. The threat of air attack brought static water tanks, which provided water to quench any fires begun by incendiary bombs, searchlight bases and air raid shelters . Although these features became a familiar part of the landscape between 1939-45, there now seems to be more evidence in the landscape of Iron Age and Medieval fortifications than of so recent a war.

Some Sources and Further Reading

BUTLER, L. *Sandal Castle, Wakefield The History and Archaeology of a Medieval Castle*, Wakefield Historical Publications, 1991.

FAULL, M. L. and MOORHOUSE, S. A. *West Yorkshire An Archaeological Survey to AD 1500 Volumes 1 to 4*, West Yorkshire Metropolitan County Council, 1981.

LE PATOUREL H.E.J. *The Moated Sites of Yorkshire*, The Society For Medieval Archaeology, 1973.

n/a *Bolling Hall, Bradford*, West Yorkshire Archaeology Service, 1988.

n/a *The Aerial Time Machine*, West Yorkshire Archaeology Service, n/d.

ORDNANCE SURVEY *1:10560 maps of Scarcroft and Scholes*, various editions.

ROBERTS, I. *Pontefract Castle*, West Yorkshire Archaeology Service, 1990.

ROBERTS, I., BURGESS, A. and BERG, D. *A New Link to the Past*, West Yorkshire Archaeology Service, 2001.

RUMSBY, J. H. *'A Castle Well Guarded'* in HAIGH E.A.H. *Huddersfield A Most Handsome Town*, Kirklees Cultural Service, 1992.

SHEERAN, G. *Brass Castles*, Ryburn, 1993.

Most of the dimensions of the features given in the text are estimates made in the field by the author.

Places to Visit

Barwick in Elmet. Walk from the remains of a moat at Scholes to Barwick in Elmet. From the graveyard observe the motte. From there, public footpaths provide excellent views of Iron Age fortifications. The walk may be extended to The Ridge (excellent view from footpath) and to Aberford but, be warned, Becca Banks are dangerous.

Bolling Hall, Bradford.

Cliffe Castle, Keighley.

Observe the moat at either **Oakwell Hall, Birstall,** or **Thornhill,** near **Dewsbury.**

Sandal Castle, Sandal. This provides a very clear understanding of the components of a medieval castle. It should be visited before looking at the ringwork and bailey at **Castle Hill, Almondbury,** and before visiting **Pontefract Castle.** Pontefract museum may also be visited.

CHURCHES AND MONUMENTS IN THE LANDSCAPE

CHURCHES OCCUR SO frequently in West Yorkshire that they can all too easily be passed by unobserved. Yet church buildings have their own history, and this chapter discusses their different architectural styles, and how they have spread across the county.

CHRONOLOGICAL CHANGES IN THE DISTRIBUTION OF CHURCHES

Too little is known about churches in Roman and sub-Roman times to enable any meaningful comment to be made about their distribution. Provided the evidence is reasonably complete, there appear to have been substantial changes in the distribution of churches during the medieval period (Figure 12.1). It seems that by the mid-eleventh century, churches were well established along the Wharfe and lower Calder valleys, and that churches were both widespread and numerous in the eastern lowlands. Perhaps this eastern concentration reflects the higher densities of population that are thought to have existed there. Many churches were built in the Pennines in the medieval period so, by 1500, churches were located in all parts of West Yorkshire, though thinly spread in the far west. This change was probably linked to an increase in the wealth and population size of the Pennines. New churches were also erected in the eastern lowlands, and this area continued to have a high density of churches (Figure 12.2).

Despite changes in religious practices brought about partly by the Reformation, there were virtually no changes in the distribution of West Yorkshire's churches between 1500 and 1650. Leeds St John's Church (1634) and a Dissenters' chapel at Bramhope (1649) are amongst the very few churches to have been erected in the county during this period. Although the Established Church was now Protestant, some of its clergy dissented from the importance placed upon the Prayer Book

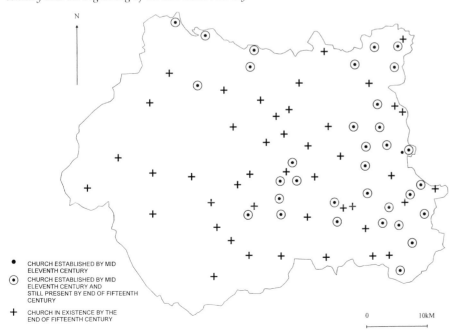

Figure 12.1. Changes in the distribution of churches in West Yorkshire, between the mid-eleventh century and the beginning of the sixteenth century.

● CHURCH ESTABLISHED BY MID ELEVENTH CENTURY

⊙ CHURCH ESTABLISHED BY MID ELEVENTH CENTURY AND STILL PRESENT BY END OF FIFTEENTH CENTURY

+ CHURCH IN EXISTENCE BY THE END OF FIFTEENTH CENTURY

0   10kM

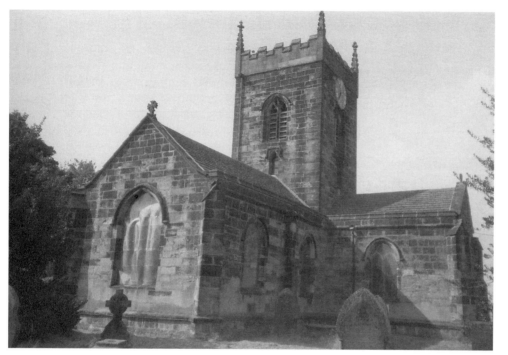

Figure 12.2. Crofton Church built c.1430. An earlier church may have existed in the Crofton area.

could openly worship, and whilst at first many met in members' homes or in barns, there soon followed a steady but slow increase in the number of Dissenters' chapels and meeting houses. The founding of new chapels accelerated in the late eighteenth century; at the same time, Methodists severed their links with the Anglican Church which led to a sharp increase in the number of Dissenters or Nonconformists.

The distribution of churches was radically altered during the nineteenth century when enormous numbers of Anglican and Nonconformist churches were built, some in areas that had previously lacked them. Nonconformists brought churches almost to the moorland edge: Congregational at Parrock Nook (1832); Wesleyan at Blackshaw Head (1815) and Baptist at Heptonstall Slack (1808), (Figure 12.3). With the opening of Heptonstall Slack chapel, residents of upper Hebden Dale were nearer than ever to a church, but were still a substantial walking distance away. To make it easier for such isolated people to attend services regularly, Heptonstall Slack Baptists erected a chapel, well up Hebden Dale, at Blake Dean. This may well have been the remotest chapel in West Yorkshire until it was demolished some thirty years ago. But other chapels remain, and even when, as at Midgley (Calderdale) and Thurstonland, they have been converted to residential use, they stand often in prominent positions and characteristically gaunt in the Pennine landscape.

in worship, and from the way the Church was organised. In 1662 large numbers of these dissenting clergy were ejected from their churches. This event was highly significant because many of those ejected, including Oliver Heywood, who had been based at Coley, illegally continued to preach, and consequently cells of Dissenters were either created or strengthened throughout the county. Other Dissenters, including Baptists and Quakers, sought independence from the Established Church. Following the *1689 Act of Toleration*, all groups of Dissenters

Figure 12.3. Heptonstall Slack Baptist Chapel, rebuilt 1878 and, to the right, its nearby, but separate, Sunday School (1863) can be seen in a moorland setting, immediately adjacent to Popples Common.

In areas of dispersed rural settlement, such as that near Heptonstall Slack, churches were, and still are, widely scattered. But in the villages, towns and cities many new churches were erected within a stone's throw of each other. Many of these then new churches were Nonconformist: by the early twentieth century the large village of Slaithwaite possessed one Anglican and six Nonconformist churches. This proliferation of churches reflected the large number of Nonconformist denominations in the nineteenth century, each of which had at least one church somewhere in West Yorkshire. It was, though, the Wesleyans and Congregationalists who made the largest contribution to the building of new chapels. Nonconformists were so successful in attracting congregations that they prompted Anglicans into building new churches of their own, and so the total stock of churches considerably increased.

Funds for these new churches came from a variety of sources. An inn-keeper lent money to Clayton Wesleyans to help them erect their chapel. Many churches were wholly or partly funded by subscriptions. The sale of burial rights and subscriptions enabled Westgate Chapel, Wakefield, to be erected in 1751-2. An 1818 Act of Parliament provided a million pounds nationally to build Anglican churches, and West Yorkshire was a major beneficiary. St Stephen's, Kirkstall was one of five Leeds churches to be built solely from state funds. Such churches are sometimes called Commissioners' churches. From 1838 the Ripon Diocesan Building Society helped fund several new Anglican churches, and many new nineteenth century churches were wholly or largely funded by wealthy industrialists. John Foster, of Black Dyke Mills, Queensbury, gave the land on which the Anglican Thornton Church is built, and the Foster family contributed to its building costs. At Meltham Mills, Charles Brook Jr. erected the Anglican St James Church in 1845 (Figure 12.4). Todmorden Unitarian Church was financed in 1865-9 by the sons of John Fielden, one of whom also erected Dobroyd Castle (chapter eleven). John

Figure 12.4. St. James Church, Meltham Mills.

Crossley of Halifax gave the land for Lightcliffe Congregational Church (1871), whilst Sir Titus Salt contributed to its building costs.

Most new nineteenth century churches were built in the growing industrial villages, towns and cities of West Yorkshire. Many of these areas are now identified as inner city areas, and it was also in these places that large numbers of Irish immigrants settled. Jewish as well as Irish immigrants made their homes in such parts of Leeds. Eventually this led to the erection of new Catholic churches and synagogues. Thirty or forty years ago, many inner city houses came to be occupied by Asians so, today, it is the large inner city areas where temples and mosques occur. Just as the Old Dissenters had initially worshipped in existing buildings, so Sikhs and Muslims changed existing buildings, including former places of worship, into temples and mosques. Later, purpose built mosques and temples have been erected. In 1999 Chapeltown Road Sikh Temple, Leeds, was built using subscriptions from the Sikh community (Figure 12.5).

Post-war immigrants were able to find homes in inner city areas because many of the indigenous people had migrated outwards to the suburbs, including to council estates. On, or close to, many of these estates new churches were erected. The Venerable Bede Wyther, built just before the Second World War and St Paul's Ireland Wood, built shortly after the war are a couple of Leeds churches erected to serve council estate residents; St Christopher's Holme Wood and St John's Thorpe Edge are two Bradford illustrations. Bishop Coggan had insisted that a church must be built in the heart of Thorpe Edge estate, but the building of St John's was a prelude to the closure, and later demolition, of Cavendish Road Church which had already existed on the periphery of the estate. Elsewhere in West Yorkshire, surplus Nonconformist chapels

Figure 12.5. Chapeltown Road Sikh Temple, Leeds.

CHURCH BUILDINGS

All the medieval churches that can be seen in West Yorkshire possess a nave and a chancel and most possess a tower (Figure 12.6). The congregation occupied the nave, whilst the chancel was the priest's preserve. Chancels came into being to provide space for an altar and rites practised by the priest. Where a tower exists, it is usually to the west of the nave, as at South Kirkby, but a few churches, including those of Kirkstall Abbey and Crofton, have a cruciform plan (Figure 12.2). The sizes of medieval church buildings range from the cathedral like grandeur of Kirkstall Abbey Church to the small chapel-of-ease at Lotherton. Medieval churches were usually built of local stone: millstone grit or sandstone in the west; limestone in the extreme east. However, Ledsham, located on Magnesian Limestone, has a lower tower of sandstone and an upper belfry of limestone. Not all medieval churches possessed a tower, but in the interest of a clear narrative, towers, spires and domes are discussed later in this section.

Following the Reformation, church designs changed, and far fewer two-roomed, nave and chancel churches were built. An exception was during the nineteenth century High Church renaissance when, from approximately 1830, many new

have been either converted to other uses, including, as at Batley, a change to a mosque, or, occasionally, demolished. For the county as a whole, though, the number of new church buildings has probably at least equalled the number destroyed. But as a result of new church buildings being erected in suburban areas, the distribution of churches changed during the twentieth century.

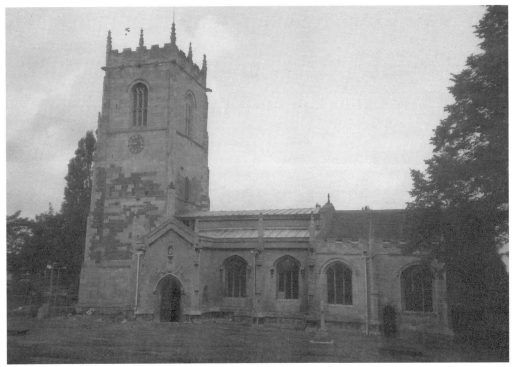

Figure 12.6. *South Kirkby Church. This church, like other medieval churches, has been subject to periodic change.*

Anglican churches, with which we are now so familiar, were built with naves and chancels. Towards the end of the nineteenth century, a few Nonconformist chapels adopted similar designs.

With these exceptions, post-Reformation churches are characterised by worship occurring in one room (Figure 12.7). The Friends had no formal services, so they simply needed a room in which to meet. For other denominations, a boxlike building became the norm (Figure 12.8). This design became so common because buildings of this type were relatively cheap to erect and met religious practices. As part of the Reformation, English rather than Latin was spoken in churches, and preaching became a most important part of the service. Broad boxlike churches were built in order to help the congregation hear the clergy. Actually, an octagonal shape offers clearer sound than a boxlike shape; but an octagonal shape is far more expensive to build. Not surprisingly, relatively few octagonal churches were built, but an eighteenth century example stands at Heptonstall (Figure 12.9). An octagonal shape also encourages members of a congregation to feel actively involved in a service. This property may have contributed to the twentieth century decisions to build octagonal worshipping areas at First Martyrs Catholic Church, Heaton, and St Paul's Anglican Church, Otley Old Road, Leeds. St Paul's parish hall is the original church building of the 1950s, and the present worshipping area was only built in 1964-65. Space for a new church building was restricted, and this may have influenced the decision to erect an octagonal worshipping area. Gomersal Wesleyan Church (1827) has a bow front design that is intermediate between the octagonal and the boxlike shape.

Figure 12.7. *Friends' Meeting House (1689), Farfield near Addingham.*

magnificent Corinthian columns. Post-Reformation churches not only reveal differences in their detailed design, but there are great differences in size and building materials. Sandstone and gritstone churches continued to be built in most parts of West Yorkshire, but brick was also used. The proportion of brick built churches was highest east of the Pennines. The nave and chancel of St Philip and St James Church, Scholes (near Cleckheaton) were built in 1876, but a century elapsed before a spire was added. By then, it was suspected the building could not support a stone spire, so one clad in fibreglass was erected.

Early Nonconformist chapels were often one tiered buildings, but by the nineteenth century, actual, or hoped for, increases in the size of a congregation had led the worshipping space of many chapels to possess a gallery and two flights of windows (Figure 12.8). Indeed, many nineteenth century churches, of whatever denomination, were large buildings, erected not only to cope with the hoped for demand, but sometimes because rooms were provided within the building for such purposes as teaching children. For similar reasons, late twentieth century purpose-built mosques and temples can be equally large buildings. Spencer Place Mosque, Leeds, not only has a large worshipping area, but has a substantial area for

Until the mid-nineteenth century, most post-Reformation churches had rather plain exteriors, and this was as true of the Anglican Commissioners' churches as it was of Nonconformist chapels. Some of the latter were enlivened by a pediment and round arched windows (Figure 12.8). In the second half of the nineteenth century, a number of Nonconformist chapels were erected with extravagant frontages, for example, the former Upper Independent Chapel at Heckmondwike possesses

Figure 12.8. Harden Congregational Church (1865).

shaped church, designed by North American architects, at Birchencliffe (near Elland) in 1965. The church was burnt down in 1992, but almost at once was re-built, again to a North American design. This time, though, the architects designed a horizontally extensive building that provides a room for worship and other rooms for basketball, drama and family history (Figure 12.10).

Large numbers of contemporary West Yorkshire churches possess one or more of a tower, spire or dome, though there are also many churches lacking these features. One of the latter is St Edmund's Roundhay where a tower, planned about a century ago, has not yet been built. The churches at Bardsey and Ledsham had effectively acquired low towers by Late Anglo-Saxon times. Perhaps these two churches were following the practice of important Anglo-Saxon lords who had chosen a tower as a status symbol. By the end of the fifteenth century, West Yorkshire's churches were characterised by their pinnacled, battlemented towers (Figure 12.6). Church towers could have become so commonplace because they enabled bells to be easily hung and enhanced the sound of bells. Church clocks developed from an early practice of using bells to summon people to worship. In late medieval times, people learnt how a clock could be used to

people to wash before entering the worshipping area, and space to train children. Chapeltown Road Sikh Temple has a vast area within the church building where people can eat, and, abutting on to the temple, is a Sikh Community Centre (Figure 12.5). Outside, as in some recently erected Christian churches, there is a large area devoted to car parking. Some Christian churches erected since 1945 are also large buildings. The Latter Day Saints erected a visually exciting vertically V-

Figure 12.9. Heptonstall Methodist Chapel (1764).

people came to own wrist watches that it was sadly deemed unnecessary to include a clock on newly built spires or towers. Certain nineteenth century Commissioners' churches, such as Pudsey St Lawrence and Dewsbury Moor St John, have towers of a medieval design, but twentieth century built towers usually lack pinnacles and embattlements, and that at The Venerable Bede Wyther, Leeds, has a particularly minimalist appearance.

Spires had been erected on the belfries of Aberford, Bramham and Ledsham Churches in medieval times. But it was not until the nineteenth century that spires became a common sight in West Yorkshire, and by that time, the then recently invented lightning conductor had made it possible for tall spires to be erected without undue risk of lightning damage. Anglicans took this opportunity to erect tall spires

strike a bell at a pre-determined time. Thereafter, between approximately the fifteenth century and the end of the nineteenth century, most towers incorporated clocks and at St Peter's Church Bramley, a clock dial was installed in each of four places around the base of the spire (Figure 12.11). When a clock was installed in Cullingworth Church tower, in 1864, sightseers were drawn from the neighbourhood to admire the huge face of the clock. During the twentieth century, so many which were considered church-like, and which would distinguish churches from warehouses, mills and, above all, Nonconformist chapels (Figures 12.8 and 12.11). However, by the end of the nineteenth century, Nonconformists were sometimes erecting spires on their newly built churches.

Churches with domes are comparatively rare in West Yorkshire, but in that late nineteenth century phase of

Figure 12.10. Birchencliffe's new Latter Day Saints Church.

Nonconformist extravagance, domes were erected on the Upper Independent Chapel at Heckmondwike and Trinity Methodist at Pudsey, although a precedent had been set at Saltaire Congregational Church in 1859. In the early twentieth century, Father O'Connor, a Catholic priest then at Heckmondwike, decided upon an eastern Mediterranean Catholic church design for his new church, and sold his collection of paintings to help pay for this domed church (Figure 12.12). It was the same Father O'Connor who decided *First Martyrs* at Heaton should have an octagonal shape.

Figure 12.11. Two of the four clock dials on the base of St Peter's Church spire, Bramley.

Figure 12.12. The Church of the Holy Spirit, Heckmondwike.

Towards the end of the twentieth century, the skyline in certain inner city areas has been cleft by minarets and domes where Muslims and Sikhs have erected mosques and temples to traditional Asian designs.

For many years churches have had a variety of functions. In some churches these functions were, and still are, accommodated within one building and, more rarely, in one room. St Margaret's Church, Newlay Lane, Leeds, (1958) is essentially a hall used on Sundays for worship and on other days occasionally hosts entertainment such as a pantomime. A similar multi-functional hall occurs at Fixby St Francis Church (1954). Often, though, the varied roles of a church have led to buildings being erected separately from the place of worship. These include huts for the uniformed organisations, parochial halls and schools. During the nineteenth century, almost all churches provided Sunday Schools and many were providers of day schools. The educational role of churches was so important because, until 1833, scarcely any other provision for the education of large numbers of poor children existed. Between 1833 and 1870, the state offered financial assistance towards the building of schools and teachers' salaries, but it was not until 1870 that state provision commenced. Some schools were accommodated inside churches, but others were held in separate buildings which were purpose-built, and often designed to indicate a connection with the church (Figure 12.13). Many of these nineteenth century school buildings remain in the landscape either occupied by businesses or, in surprisingly large numbers, by schools.

Figure 12.13. Darrington Church of England School.

MONUMENTS

Monuments are widely scattered throughout West Yorkshire. At any one locality there may be just one individual monument, but at cemeteries many monuments occur clustered together. Prior to the nineteenth century, a comparatively low population size meant there was usually adequate space to bury the dead in church graveyards. This was no longer true, in the nineteenth century, in those areas of rapid town growth which also had a large number of deaths. Consequently, local councils, for example at Beckett Street, Leeds, (1845) and private companies, for example, at Undercliffe, Bradford, (1854) began to create cemeteries on sites away from existing churches. Churches to provide funeral services were erected in a number of cemeteries, but the landscape of a cemetery is dominated by its monuments. Headstones, table tombs and obelisks are common types of monument, and are each visible in Heptonstall Methodist burial ground (Figure 12.9). There are variations, from cemetery to cemetery, in the proportion of different kinds of monument, and in their spatial arrangement. The Friends' burial grounds at Rawdon and Scholes (near Cleckheaton) are a regiment of headstones, each about one metre high. At Scholes these are evenly distributed, whilst at Rawdon the headstones are arranged in parallel lines. Equality in death is unique to The Friends' burial grounds. Even the virtually identical headstones of the Beckett Street Guinea Graves (1879-1930) display slight contrasts in their summit carvings, and their near uniformity reflects the standard price paid by the deceased's family, rather than religious tenet (Figure 12.14). Moreover, within nineteenth century burial grounds, sharp

Figure 12.14. Guinea Graves, Beckett Street Cemetery, Leeds.

Individual monuments include the Ellis Memorial Clock Tower, Norwood Green, the obelisk in St Ives Park erected to commemorate WB Ferrand and a stone post to Matt Dodgson who bequeathed a field to the poor of Thorner; but by far the most numerous of West Yorkshire's individual monuments are war memorials. Virtually every community grieved the death of some of its members during the Great War, so virtually every community has its war memorial. Usually the names of people killed on active service in the Second World War were carved on to the Great War memorials. Monuments to civilians killed by enemy action are uncommon, but along Went Lane, between Fitzwilliam and Purston Jaglin, a monument solely to the 1940 victims of a delayed action bomb has been erected (Figure 12.15b)). And those Leeds residents who died in German air raids in the 1939-45 war are commemorated by a small stone monument, unveiled in 2003, at Rosebank Millennium Green. One war memorial rises prominently above a bench close to New Bridge (Hebden Dale); another, at Streethouse, lies neglected by a railway line; yet others are by roadsides. Many war memorials are located in town and city centres; some are in church yards and others are in parks. The designs of war memorials are equally varied, ranging from the grandeur of that in Greenhead Park, Huddersfield, to the simplicity of the small monument by the side of Went Lane (12.15). Small monuments have been erected at Adwalton Moor to remind visitors of a 1643 Civil War Battle which was won by the Royalists. British success in the Napoleonic Wars was commemorated in Calderdale by the erection of a tall monument at Stoodley Pike. Soon after being struck by lightning in 1854 the original monument collapsed, the 1856 replacement being thirty seven metres high. Both the height of the monument, and its site on an elevated remnant of an erosion surface, make it such a prominent Pennine landmark.

contrasts exist between low headstones, and more ornate and towering monuments which relate to the amount of money families could afford, or were prepared to pay, for monuments. In some cemeteries the different types of monument can occur mixed together, but at Undercliffe Cemetery an area of smoke-blackened headstones is followed by a linear zone of tall, visually impressive monuments which culminate in a very tall obelisk that overlooks most of Bradford. Clustered just to the north of this zone are the low, but by no means uniform, headstones of recent burials.

(a)

(b)

Figure 12.15. *Contrasts in War Memorials (a) Greenhead Park (b) Along Went Lane.*

Whilst many monuments have been erected to commemorate wars and the dead, some monuments have been erected to mark peaceful occasions and certain types of work. The clock tower by Otley Market Place was erected to celebrate Queen Victoria's Golden Jubilee in 1887. It had first been intended to raise funds to build a cottage hospital and make a recreation ground. However, the amount of money collected proved insufficient to provide even one these amenities let alone two. It was only after some vacillation that a decision was taken to use some of the funds to erect a clock tower. Queen Victoria's sixty years as monarch, in 1897, was recognised by the erection of one tower at Steeton and another at Castle Hill, Almondbury (Figure 11.3). In sharp contrast, a monument at South Kirkby is low and far from impressive, yet, from its presence, one can imagine the delight that councillors

Figure 12.16. *Monument to the mine workers of Sharlston Colliery.*

experienced when the local coal mining economy was diversified by the 1949 opening of the Langthwaite Grange Industrial Estate. Many former coal mining villages in the Wakefield district display half of a wheel that was once part of a nearby pit head mining gear (Figure 12.16). These half-wheels are monuments to former mining communities, but they are also monuments to that instrument of landscape change: coal itself.

Some Sources and Further Reading

BARNARD, S. M. *To Prove I'm Not Forgot,* Manchester University Press, 1990.

BIELBY, A. R. *Churches and Chapels of Kirklees,* Kirklees Metropolitan Council, 1978.

DALTON, H. W. *Anglican Resurgence under W. F. Hook in Early Victorian Leeds,* The Thoresby Society, 2002.

FAULL, M. L. and MOORHOUSE, S. A. *West Yorkshire An Archaeological Survey to AD 1500 Volumes 1 to 4,* West Yorkshire Metropolitan County Council, 1981.

JOWITT, J. A. *Model Industrial Communities in Mid-Nineteenth Century Yorkshire,* University of Bradford, 1986.

MORRIS, R. K. *Churches in the Landscape,* Dent, 1989.

RYDER, P. *Medieval Churches of West Yorkshire,* West Yorkshire Archaeology Service, 1993.

SILSON, A. *Religious Roles In The Nineteenth Century Social Growth Of Bramley* in Stevenson Tate L *Aspects of Leeds. 2,* Wharncliffe, 1999.

STELL, C. *Nonconformist Chapels and Meeting Houses in the North of England,* HMSO, 1994.

Places to Visit

Short Tours

1. Everyone should visit Kirkstall Abbey, Leeds. From the Abbey, a tour can be taken to the north to include two former Methodist chapels, St Stephen's Church and The Church of the Latter-Day Saints, Hawksworth.
2. From St Paul's Church (on Otley Old Road, Leeds) to Adel Church (with its fine Norman doorway) and then, if on foot, over the fields to Eccup and thence to Bramhope to observe its 1649 chapel.
3. From Undercliffe Cemetery to Eccleshill (1775 Methodist Chapel) to St John's, Thorpe Edge; various churches in Idle may then be observed en route to Westfield Lane to The Friends Burial Ground.

Individual Churches (Church of England unless otherwise stated)

Either **Bardsey** or **Ledsham** (Ledsham Church is probably the oldest building in West Yorkshire).

Either **Batley** to observe a cluster of Mosques in the Purlwell Lane district or **Leeds** to observe Chapeltown Road Sikh Temple and Spencer Place Mosque.

Bramham, particularly to observe its large graveyard which may be of pre-conquest age.

Crofton.

Farfield, near Addingham: Friends Meeting House.

Heckmondwike: 1. The former Upper Independent Chapel and Sunday School. 2. The Church of the Holy Spirit.

Heptonstall Methodist Chapel.

Heptonstall Slack Baptist Chapel and Sunday School.

Kirkheaton. As well as the church, observe the monument to the seventeen children who died in a fire at Atkinson's Mill in 1818.

Lotherton Chapel.

Meltham Mills to observe St James' Church and nearby former National School.

Otley; notice the monument, near the graveyard, to the workers killed whilst erecting Bramhope Tunnel.

Saltaire Congregational Church.

Scholes (near Cleckheaton). 1. St Philip and St James Church. 2. Friends Meeting House and burial ground.

South Kirkby or **Walton** (near Wetherby).

Stanley: Commissioners' Church of unusual design.